Books by Morris Bishop

CHAMPLAIN: THE LIFE OF FORTITUDE

THE LIFE AND ADVENTURES OF LA ROCHEFOUCAULD

PETRARCH AND HIS WORLD

PASCAL: THE LIFE OF GENIUS

THE HORIZON BOOK OF THE MIDDLE AGES

THE ODYSSEY OF CABEZA DE VACA

RONSARD: PRINCE OF POETS

A HISTORY OF CORNELL

A BOWL OF BISHOP

As editor

A CLASSICAL STORYBOOK

A MEDIEVAL STORYBOOK

A RENAISSANCE STORYBOOK

A ROMANTIC STORYBOOK

A SURVEY OF FRENCH LITERATURE

A TREASURY OF BRITISH HUMOR

As translator

EIGHT PLAYS OF MOLIÈRE

LETTERS FROM PETRARCH

The
Library
of World
Biography

Saint Francis
of Assisi

By Morris Bishop

THE LIBRARY OF WORLD BIOGRAPHY

J. H. PLUMB, GENERAL EDITOR

Little, Brown and Company—Boston—Toronto

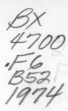

FIRST EDITION

T 11/74

*The frontispiece is from a painting
of Saint Francis of Assisi by Cimabue.*

LIBRARY OF CONGRESS CATALOGING IN PUBLICATION DATA

Bishop, Morris, 1893–1973.
    St. Francis of Assisi.

    Bibliography: p.
    1. Francesco d'Assisi, Saint, 1182–1226.
BX4700. F6 B52   1974   282:092'4[B]   74–10757
ISBN 0–316–09665–2

*Published simultaneously in Canada
by Little, Brown & Company (Canada) Limited*

PRINTED IN THE UNITED STATES OF AMERICA

Introduction

WHEN WE LOOK BACK at the past nothing, perhaps, fascinates us so much as the fate of individual men and women. The greatest of these seem to give a new direction to history, to mold the social forces of their time and create a new image, or open up vistas that humbler men and women never imagined. An investigation of the interplay of human temperament with social and cultural forces is one of the most complex yet beguiling studies a historian can make; men molded by time, and time molded by men. It would seem that to achieve greatness both the temperament and the moment must fit like a key into a complex lock. Or rather a master key, for the very greatest of men and women resonate in ages distant to their own. Later generations may make new images of them — one has only to think what succeeding generations of Frenchmen have made of Napoleon, or Americans of Benjamin Franklin — but this only happens because some men change the course of history and stain it with their own ambitions, desires, creations or hopes of a magnitude that embraces future generations like a miasma. This is particularly true of the great figures of religion, of politics, of war. The great creative spirits, however, are used by subsequent generations in a reverse manner — they go to them to seek hope or solace, or to confirm despair, reinterpreting the works of imagination or wisdom to ease them in their own desperate necessities, to beguile them with a sense of beauty or merely to draw from them strength and understanding. So this series of biographies tries in lucid, vivid, and dramatic narratives to explain the greatness of men and women, not only how they managed to secure their niche in the great pantheon of Time, but also why they have continued to fascinate subsequent generations. It may seem, therefore, that it is paradoxical for this series to contain living men and women, as well as the dead, but it is not so. We can recognize, in our own time, particularly in those whose careers are getting close to their final hours, men and women of indisputable greatness, whose position in history is secure, and about whom the legends and myths are beginning to sprout — for all great men and women become legends, all become in history larger than their own lives.

Different times, different men. It is rare to find a saint in the modern world, but the Middle Ages had a deep and constant need for men and women who could suffer intensely, carry the burdens of mankind, yet radiate with the joy of God. It is hard for us to grasp how easily human lives were broken with tragedy in the Middle Ages. Italy, as medieval countries went, was comparatively richer, both in the produce of the land and in the commerce of its cities. Yet great sections of the population lived on the very margin of subsistence, just not hungry in times of good harvests, starving in bad. And the same was true of the workers that crowded some of the cities such as Florence. When there was plenty of work and cheap food, they could live tolerably; less work and high prices, their lives and their children's lives were at risk. Equally uncertain was the visitation of plague or diseases that swept through Italy and killed and killed until they burned themselves out like a forest fire. Sometimes the cattle died, rather than the people; the result was equally devastating. And if it was not plague, it might be war; violent bands of men who had no mercy for a peasant. They could kill for pleasure, as well as for necessity.

Nor was it entirely a world of poverty, pain and disease. There were many rich people — nobles, merchants, bankers — who never starved, who could escape from the plague-ridden towns to their villas, who took delight in the physical luxuries of the world, in the lust of life and the pride of the eye, and believed that this vivid contrast of pain and suffering, ease and delight, was God's will. All was ordained. Hard, at times, that might be to believe. And very hard, indeed, to believe at times of the Church — popes and cardinals living as richly as sovereign princes, monks and nuns taking their ease and contentment, not mortified by mankind's suffering.

But such a world was as terrible as an open wound to some men and women of deep compassion — of whom Saint Francis was one. Born to comfort and a world of ease; he rejected both — embraced poverty, disease, suffering, with ecstasy and joy. And so he caught the imagination of the world that had to believe that the weak, the sick, the hungry would inherit heaven, that there was virtue in suffering. And in his own lifetime Saint Francis became a mythic figure, curing the sick, feeding the hungry, gloating almost in his own pain as a precious gift of God. He reidentified the Christmas message in a vivid human way with the teaching of Christ. Also he managed — just — to stay within the confines of the Catholic Church, and therefore helped to generate one of its periods of reform and renewal. He and his little band of brothers, and his sister, Saint Claire, lived haphazardly the life of religious ecstasy and practice. But he, too, had his Saint Paul in Brother Elias, who formalized the movement, turning Saint Francis into the Franciscans — one of the great crusading powers of the late Middle Ages.

And so the story of Saint Francis illuminates so many facets of life: the deeper springs of the human spirit, as well as the desperate nature of his times.

— J. H. PLUMB

Contents

Saint Francis of Assisi

ONE

Assisi 1182

ASSISI, THE SERAPHIC CITY, is an enormous reliquary, to
be adored rather than loved. The barefoot pilgrim climbs
a weary way to her; the idle tourist may feel himself an
awkward intruder on her sanctity. She looks a fossil city,
deposited by time, not built. But her grimness is lightened by the rosy tint of her limestone, by the rare green
bloom in the shaded loggias.

Assisi is ancient indeed. She goes back to the Umbrians,
before the Etruscans came and then the Romans. Her
name apparently meant "altar, erected to the rising sun."
She should properly be called Oriente, says Dante, for
from her came the Dayspring from on high which hath
visited us. Her citizens are very conscious of past time
and of time to come. They are stoic-trained, having
learned to suffer and endure in a nearly vertical world,
wherein the least errand demands the ascent of a hundred stone steps. Many streets and passages, the width of a
pack-saddled mule, are still medieval, save only for droops
of electric wiring or a motor scooter asleep against a wall.

The Assisans are conscious custodians of a reliquary. No house can be built, no stone moved, without the consent of the civic guardians. Fidelity is to the citizens' interest; piety and miracle provide their bread and oil. The Assisans are not lovers of Lady Poverty; good Brother Francis has bequeathed them comfort and prosperity. They are grateful; they know that their city exists only by grace of Saint Francis.

Assisi is a tiny city to be so famous, but it is larger than Bethlehem, as large as Nazareth. Censuses showed a population of 4,900 in 1656, of 3,705 in 1881; now it is reckoned at about 10,000. In the time of Saint Francis the walls bounded half the present area; the inhabitants, however medievally crowded, could hardly have exceeded today's numbers. The reader should picture a small town, with the typical character of the small town, puffed with local pride and scorn of the outsider, but inwardly itching with rivalries and jealousies. Everyone knew everyone's business. Leagues, factions, groupings of kinship, class, interest, hatred, flourished.

The reader should be aware likewise of the time — the closing years of the twelfth century. What we have chosen to call the Dark Ages were past, and western Europe was emerging into what we have chosen to call the High Middle Age. In central Italy, at least, people had gained a relative prosperity. The restraints of law were imposed on noble brigands; peace and stability generally reigned, and as a result population increased, land was more intensively tilled, the Church established hospitals and social services and drew on the people to build magnificent churches. A certain modicum of ease and comfort came to be among the well-to-do. Poverty, of course, continued to exist; but even the poor seem to have had enough to eat and adequate shelter, with a little surplus for almsgiving for the desperate. We shall see that Francis and his companions, poorest among the poor, seldom returned empty-handed from their begging excursions.

The world of ideas, upon which modern historians linger lovingly, was inaccessible to the average man of 1182. Few could read, fewer knew Latin, yet fewer could deal with abstract concepts. But all together accepted some fundamental ideas. First, the truth of Christian doctrine, comporting a theology, cosmology, science, history, and promise or threat of a future life, with its rewards and punishments. This doctrine, incorporating remnants of ancient paganism, systematized by the Church and promulgated by parish priests, answered all a simple man's questions.

Second, the average man accepted that he lived in a world of miracle. He did not distinguish between natural and supernatural. The vagaries of weather, storm and drought, epidemic diseases, the favor or hostility of chance, the bounty or malevolence of nature, even birth and death, could only be explained as the work of conscious powers, saints and demons. These powers heard their prayers, and responded with pity or anger. The simple man needed saints. They had been his adored companions on earth, and they lobbied for him in the forecourts of Heaven. He also needed devils, for without them he could hardly explain the problem of evil.

Third, the average man held that the right of property ownership was fundamental. The peasant with his hoe, the knight with his sword, the bishop with his crook — all proclaimed: "This is mine! Mine by right!" The idea of property ownership was basic in the great dispute which runs through most of medieval history — the dispute between pope and emperor as to the limits of their power and possessions. The contest was about an equal one. The emperor had his armies drawn from savage lands beyond the Alps; he had his powerful allies, and sometimes even the strength of unfaith. The pope was fortified by his own sacred character, an organization covering Christendom, access to colossal wealth, and weapons of damnation in his hand.

The Lombards, mostly German and naturally the emperor's men, had long since taken over northern Italy and moved south into Umbria. There they planted German feudalism, a fine system for ruling a farm country, but ill adapted to managing commercial cities. In Assisi, as elsewhere, the nobles lost control of the city, which became governmentally a commune, a republic. In our year 1182 it still owed nominal allegiance to the German duke of Spoleto, but even this was annulled later, when the duke was forced to surrender his territories to Pope Innocent III. In 1198 the young men of Assisi sacked the duke's castle above the city; sixteen-year-old Francis could very well have joined the attackers.

The nobles, largely German or of Germanic stock, were resolutely Ghibelline, partisans of the emperor, while the commoners were Guelf, faithful to the pope. The conflict between Guelf and Ghibelline filled the times, and set city against city, family against family. (A convenient mnemonic aid — "Guelf" and "pope" are monosyllables, "Ghibelline" and "emperor" trisyllables.)

The Ghibelline nobles of Assisi represented a losing, even a lost, cause. Having lost control of the city, they retreated to their country castles, complaining of reduced income, of vanished power, of reluctant service by an insolent peasantry. The new rulers — free burghers, merchants, notaries and such — forced the gentry to maintain town residences and to occupy them for a part of the year. There the grumbling gentlemen could be watched, and seized as hostages in case of trouble. The clever money-men and law-men nibbled away at the old feudal rights and bought in the war-men's lands at forced sales. All this sounds very familiar, even normal, to us who have watched many revolutions of the Wheel of Fortune. But the nobles knew no history; they thought that the end of the world had come. As their importance dwindled their arrogance increased.

Socially the nobles continued to dominate, for it was understood that a bluer blood ran in their veins than in those of common folk. The clergy shared their prestige, thanks to their intimacy with higher powers; also, the higher clergy were likely to be chosen from noble stock. The clergy were marked, by character and training, as a separate class, recognizable by their tonsure and sober dress — although a uniform habit was required only of the monks. The clerics were subject to their own hierarchy, ruled by their own courts. In faraway Rome the Church was riddled with venality, simony (the purchase and sale of Church offices), corruption, but in Assisi the clergy seem to have been pious and clean-living. Much depended on the local bishop and his staff, and Assisi was blessed with a series of worthy prelates against whom no evil was alleged. True, heresy and near-heresy were rife. The visionary prophecies of Joachim of Flora, the Manichaean doctrines of the Cathari, or Patarenes, the rejection of property ownership by the Waldensians, or Poor Men of Lyons, tempted many, not by promises of moral relaxation but by resentment of clerical abuses and by a widespread yearning for a stricter and purer rule of life. The strength of the reform movement lay with the artisans — weavers, tailors, cutlers and such — who had time to think and talk at their sedentary labors. Even in Assisi, traditionally orthodox, a heretic *podestà,* or mayor, was elected in 1203.

Socially inferior to the nobles and higher clergy were the merchants, the bourgeois. Most of these had emerged from the little people, the *popolo minuto,* or their fathers had done so before them. They were the shrewd, the bold, the risk-takers, the eternal Businessmen. The nobles detested the merchants, and were repaid by the merchants' detestation. The feudal nobles measured consideration in land, the merchants in money, and now the economy was shifting from a land base to a money base. The nobles, hard pressed for cash, sold off bits of their land; it was snapped up by the merchants, who thus sought both profit and the consideration due to landed proprietors.

Below the merchants were ranged the artisans, the laborers, servants, common folk of all sorts, with the beggars at the bottom. Though the commoners greatly outnumbered their betters, they could exert an influence only by mass demonstrations and riots, which seldom succeeded. In the story of Saint Francis they are merely background figures.

At all these social levels national feeling, Italian patriotism, did not exist, but local loyalty was almost unbelievably strong. A man was bound to his city by an unseverable bond. Even Petrarch, born in exile from his ancestral Florence, who saw his father-town only twice, and briefly, always proudly proclaimed himself a Florentine. The city demanded obedience, loyalty, even love. A man belonged to a group or several groups, but the sum total of the groups made up the city-state. It could establish unity under threats from without, and fall again to civil broils when danger dwindled. The horizontal levels of society were crossed by many vertical sectionings. The citizen "belonged for his entire life to a determined class, to a trade, to a corporation, a parish, a quarter," wrote Emile Gebhard a century ago.

His consuls and councils not only assigned him his share of political liberty, but regulated by decree the acts of his private life, prescribing the number of fig and almond trees he might plant in his field, the number of priests and tapers that should attend his funeral, forbade him to enter into taverns reserved for foreigners, to give presents to newly-married couples, to wear jewels or precious stuffs beyond a certain value; if he was a barber, to shave for more than a penny; if a rope-maker, to work on wet days; if a huntsman, to catch quails otherwise than in a snare; if a fisherman, to sell his fish outside the city; and if he were a farmer he was commanded to bring to the commune the corn he did not himself consume. Air and sunlight alone seem to have escaped this regulation of individual rights.

Assisi's principal business was in wool and woolens. The commerce was international. Sellers of raw wool from England, processors from the Low Countries, buyers from Italy, importers of luxury materials from the East, met at the spring fairs, chiefly in the Champagne country of France. They talked styles, qualities and prices, sold and bought, amused themselves, and returned with loaded mule trains over specified, well-policed trade routes. The French road, *via francesca,* passed near Assisi; dealers even from the Orient trod its course on their way north from Bari or another seaport to Florence, the Alpine passes, and Champagne.

Eminent among the Assisan cloth merchants was Pietro Bernardone.* We know nothing of his background; probably he or his father had fought his way up from poverty. He certainly showed the pride of a self-made man. He was rich, even very rich, *praedivus.* An early writer, perhaps blackening the father the better to glorify the son, calls him sly and violent. No doubt; he was, on the evidence, forceful, obstinate, clever, practical. Several times at least he made the long buyers' journey to Champagne. He conceived a certain cult for France. His wife, Madonna Pica, was the daughter of a rich merchant; it is surmised that she was French, for no better reason than that her un-Italian name, Pica, suggests Picardy. But *pica* in Italian means "magpie," and maybe she was nicknamed for her chattering. The early writer calls her simple and kind. Those are easy, inevitable adjectives; she was type-cast, to be the figure of Holy Motherhood.

Pietro Bernardone's combined home and shop stood near the center of the city. The exact location is bitterly argued in Assisi. In whatever case, the space for storage and display of goods and for family life was extremely narrow. Certainly Pietro did not gain his wealth from selling cloth. As there were no banks in Assisi, he obliged the improvident by lending them money at handsome rates of interest, and he profited by foreclosing on delin-

---

* We pause here a moment to speak of Italian names in the twelfth century. Usually only a gentleman of rank would bear a family name. Others had a Christian name followed by *di* plus the father's Christian name, or, more rarely, by a suffix such as *-one* added to the father's name. A man might also be named by his place of origin, preceded by *da.* Our Francis would normally have been called Francesco di Pietro; he preferred Francesco Bernardone, following his father in arrogating to himself, with a hint of gentility, a family name.

quent debtors' property. Thus he came to hold a half-dozen small country acreages, with their vineyards, grain fields, and olive groves, supplying his table with fresh vegetables and conferring on him the status of land-holder. Like many another local businessman he was ready to invest in any good visible security. Though he made many enemies in his ascent, he was public-spirited and gave lavishly to municipal good works. He gained the respect of Assisi's solid citizens and had every reason to be satisfied with his own dealings and reputation, proud of his success.

In his Assisan home there was a son, Angelo, possibly other children, who, if they existed, are never mentioned in the story. Some time in 1182 Madonna Pica gave birth to another son. She proposed to name the newcomer John-Baptist. But her husband, on his return from a business trip to France, overruled her. It was generally believed that a name had a profound influence on char-acter, and the influence of John the Baptist — recluse, her-mit, fanatic, locust-eater dressed in a camel's skin — was of ill augury for a cloth merchant. Pietro Bernardone decreed that the boy's name should be Francesco, the Frenchman, "Frenchy," an unusual given name, but one suggesting frankness, freedom. It was not absolutely unique; earnest researchers, examining four thousand names recorded at Pistoia in 1219, discovered thirteen Francescos among them. Said Tommaso da Celano, Fran-cis's devoted follower: "The rarity and singularity of his name must have aided much in the rapid success of his work in the world." But there was then no San Francesco in heaven to be his patron and advocate, so he filled the niche himself, to be the patron of all the Francescos, Franks, Franzes and Françoises who have succeeded him.

TWO

Young Francesco Bernardone

AT THE PROPER TIME young Francesco Bernardone was
sent to the clergy of San Giorgio, his parish church, to
learn his letters and the ciphering necessary for a merchant. He sat on a bench with the better-class boys,
chorusing sacred Latin. He was not a brilliant student.
The three extant scraps of his writing betray a clumsy
fist and abound in sad solecisms. In later years he avoided
holding the pen; he preferred to dictate, and to sign his
pronouncements with a cross or tau, a semisacred symbol.
However, he learned enough Latin for his purposes, for
school routine and for the comprehension of the ritual.
He had a good voice and probably sang in the choir,
mastering the noble language of the anthems and hymns.
And, surely with his father's encouragement, he gained a
fluent knowledge of both French and Provençal. He did
not read French literature, of course, for he would have
had no access to profane books, but he may well have
listened entranced to wandering minstrels, refugees from
Albigensian persecutions, who sang in the marketplaces

their songs of love and chanted tales of knighthood and adventure.

He had also the education of the home and shop. He could admire his father, honest and worthy, but an austere man, taking up where he laid not down, reaping where he had not sown. Pietro Bernardone demanded all his rights and legal dues. Francis learned to appreciate the colors and qualities of cloth; he could applaud the drama of successful selling. He must have witnessed the anger and tears of distrained debtors, smitten by seizures and foreclosures. Sensitive as he was, he must have been moved to pity without actually blaming his father.

At fourteen Francis was formally apprenticed to the family concern; he surrendered his freedom and most of his waking hours to his duties. Though he was called a good businessman, he was soon bored by the drudgery of cleaning, mending, displaying, and recording, and he suffered from the reproofs of his father and his brother Angelo. What he enjoyed was the choice of the richest, most scintillating materials for his own adornment. Being a joker, he delighted in confecting bizarre costumes, patching the coarsest sackcloth with the most expensive fancy goods in the shop. He was, simply, fond of dressing up, of playing a part. That was the troubadour in him, acting in an extemporized drama.

The drama rendered his secret dream, the realization of the chivalrous life. The exploits of Charlemagne's paladins and the Knights of the Round Table were already familiar throughout Italy, and the code of knightly behavior was known and honored, if little practiced. The proper knight undertook to right wrongs, protect the weak, defend churchmen, widows, and orphans, and humble himself before his Lady. Francis's imagination disported itself in the enchanted world of knighthood; and all his life he used the language of chivalry and appealed to its ideals. He sang like a troubadour; he undertook many a perilous quest. When the time came he groveled before his Lady — but his Lady was unique. She was the Lady Poverty — the most unwelcome of guests in the Bernardone household.

What did Francis look like? All our descriptions are from later periods, but through them we may perceive the adolescent of Assisi. All the reporters agree that he was short, dark-skinned, unhandsome, mean-looking. Cimabue's portrait in the Assisi basilica, not done from life, shows a grubby weasely face above a thin, shoulderless body. Tommaso da Celano gives us a full description.

> He was of middle height, rather short than tall. His skull was round, of ordinary dimensions, his face a little elongated, the brow short and straight, the eyes of medium size, black and limpid, the hair dark, the eyebrows straight, the nose regular, narrow, upright, the ears small, seeming to be always listening, the temples flat. His manner of speech was soothing, burning, and penetrating, his voice vibrant and sweet, clear and sonorous. His teeth were close-set, regular, white, his lips thin and narrow, his beard black and straggling, his neck thin. His shoulders were straight, his arms short, with small hands and delicate fingers and prominent nails. His legs were thin, his feet small, his skin soft. He bore the very minimum of flesh.

True, the several descriptions are of Francis worn out by privations and mistreatment of the body, but they bear out a spectator who heard Francis preach in Bologna in

1222 and who reported that his person was unimpressive, his face unlovely.

As a boy, he must have been distressed by the niggardly gifts of nature. He compared his own thin biceps with those of his playmates, young gentlemen mostly of German stock, bred to roughness and toughness, ready with fist and sword, trained to noble arrogance. He invented an insecure arrogance of his own, trying to outdo his companions in follies and display. According to Tommaso da Celano, he was brought up in insensate luxury and was encouraged to lewd behavior from childhood on. At the very least, this statement seems to falsify the character of mother and father. Pietro Bernardone had worked hard for his money; he would have had no patience with lewd behavior, which is bound to be expensive. More credible is the record of another writer, who echoes household upbraidings: "His parents reproached him much for spending money on himself and others, saying that to look at him you'd think him the son of a prince, not of a merchant!" The phrase still carries the rhythm of parental reproof, and pride of place, not envy. When Pietro Bernardone saw his son in a costume of his own devising, a bizarre patchwork, he fell into a rage. The boy bade fair to ruin him, and to ruin his elder brother as well! But the father may well have felt a grumbling satisfaction that his son was so popular among the young gentry. When a friend of noble family came to summon Francis in midmeal, the boy immediately rose and went off with his companion. Pietro swore at his son's unmannerly behavior and snobbishness, but he was something of a snob himself. And Francis could mollify his father, mollify almost anyone, by the exercise of his mysterious charm. He could disarm and captivate, whether consciously or unconsciously. We see him employing his youthful charm to cajole his family and friends; we shall see it grow until it contains a world in its spell.

If the hagiographers tell the truth — why should they not, indeed? — Francis felt already the stir of charity, the pull of pity. Our legend records that he was one day busy at his tasks in the shop when a poor man came in and asked for alms, for the love of God. At first Francis brushed off the beggar; then, suddenly touched by divine grace, he reproached himself for his harshness, reflecting, "If this beggar had asked you for something in the name of some grandee, count or baron, certainly you would have received his request graciously. So all the more should you do so for the King of Kings and Lord of Lords." He therefore resolved that in the future he would grant what might be asked of him in the name of the greatest master.

Tommaso da Celano deplores Francis's wasted years and steps aside, but his strictures reveal an unwilling admiration, even envy.

Superior to all his comrades on the head of frivolity, he was the life and soul of their parties. He excited them to evil and tried to outdo them in folly. He dazzled them all, and tried to distinguish himself in demonstrations of vainglory — games, farces, buffooneries, jokes, songs — while wearing garments soft and delicate. He was very rich, in fact, but by no means stingy; on the contrary, he was lavish. He was a good businessman but was willing to spend foolishly. He had great personal charm, and was winning in conversation; and this, alas, merely favored his folly by assembling about him a collection of young men of bad behavior and vicious habits. One often saw him, surrounded by his unworthy band, magnificent, with his head held high, parading through the high streets of Babylon.

Worshipers of the saint, outraged by this passage, have been wont to dismiss it as merely a literary imitation of Saint Augustine, who also deplores his missteps in the high streets of Babylon. It is alleged that Tommaso's lurid picture is an effort to dramatize Francis's virtues in maturity by contrast with the wicked society of his youth. But Arnaldo Fortini, paragon of researchers, has discovered in the Assisan archives many facts about Francis's club. It was called "the Company of the Tripudiantes," the joyful dancers, the caper-cutters. Its stated purpose was to dance in public. The master of the dance, keeping time with a ceremonial wand, sang a familiar ballad, and the participants, men and women, followed, holding one another by the hand and executing their traditional steps and capers. Far from being licentious, the dances were likely to represent scenes from sacred history. At the end, the thirsty performers proceeded to a sumptuous banquet, and ended by clattering down the city streets, to the annoyance of all sober folk.

We are not told the names of the participants in the frolics. Presumably they were the young nobles, whose parents felt it their duty to live with *magnificenza,* whether they could afford it or not. Merchants' sons, even if socially acceptable to the club members, found their fathers unwilling to dip into their money hoards to pay for such foolishness. But Francis came as a savior. The club had a convenient rule: the master of the feast designated a member who would pay the entire cost of the banquet, and in all decency he would designate himself. Francis could be depended on to assume the charges, pick up the tab. He was repaid by enthusiastic acclaim, by a most obvious popularity; but did he recognize that the impecunious young nobles regarded him as what can only be called a sucker?

Who, one wonders, were the lady dancers performing in the stony streets of Assisi? Not, certainly, the yet un-married daughters of the nobility; these were kept in al-most Oriental seclusion. Nor were they the young wives of gentlemen, for typically a noble marriage united a middle-aged knight and a girl barely nubile; the husband would not have approved a public gambol with a miscel-laneous lot of commoners and worse. And even a young husband, cherishing Italian jealousies and suspicions, would have considered the Company of Tripudiantes not quite the milieu for his wife. The female dancers must have been demimondaines, the light-o'-loves of the young gentlemen. But how many demimondaines could a town of ten thousand support? Arnoldo Fortini has turned up several in the records — Brunetta, Letizia, Colata, Grazia, Amata, Matarosa, Fidanza, and a horrible Berta Olivana, called the she-wolf, who made her headquarters in an underground tomb. Such were Francis's companions, well known to the police. They were no vestals, certainly.

And Francis? We are not the first to be inquisitive about his sex life. His faithful follower, Brother Leo, was tormented by the question of whether Francis had lost his virginity, and was assured by divine revelation of the saint's immaculateness. "The flesh which was to re-ceive the stigmata was preserved from the defilement of carnal sin." Saint Bonaventure himself asserts that Saint Francis went not astray in surrender to the sins of the flesh. Bernard of Besse, Bonaventure's secretary, roundly

calls Francis a virgin till death. But Saint Francis, in
his Testament, speaks of the time when "I was still
dwelling in sin." What does he mean by that? For the
medieval cleric, sexual commerce was the sin par excel-
lence, the devil's favorite enticement and trap. One may
picture, if one will, fastidious young Francis holding
aloof from his club of loose-living youths and their wantons; but one may just as well presume that, unless
Italians have markedly changed, he indulged his lust and
appeased his youthful curiosity.

After all, the matter is one of very small importance.

Matters of much greater moment than Francis's virginity were agitating the world. The German Henry VI,
son of Frederick Barbarossa, succeeded his father as Roman emperor in 1191, and was himself succeeded by
Otto IV in 1209. In 1187 Jerusalem, after a century in
Christian hands, fell to Sultan Saladin. In 1198 the
Fourth Crusade was declared, that wicked crusade that
ravished Christian Constantinople. But in such high
matters Francis showed no interest. The one great affair
that eventually concerned him was the election of Pope
Innocent III, the Church reformer, the daunter of kings
and emperors, in 1198.

Another affair, not so great, intruded upon his private
life, and changed his purposes and perhaps his character.
This was the war with Perugia.

Perugia stands only fifteen miles westward of Assisi.
It was and is a proud city, boasting that it is the beloved
daughter of Rome. It continues to build and grow with
Roman ruthlessness. It looks impregnable on its hilltop,
behind its Etruscan walls. Its population in 1200 was
several times that of Assisi, and it commanded a larger
and more prosperous territory. The boundary between

the two little states was marked by the stripling Tiber. Ghibelline Perugia hated Guelf Assisi, and was cordially hated in return. The citizens were frequent visitors to one another's streets in the way of business, and they revealed their lack of assurance by their truculent airs. Offense was quickly given, as quickly taken. The background of *Romeo and Juliet* could readily be transplanted to Perugia. The armed guards of the gentlemen swaggered before the out-of-town civilians, as soldiers always have; the sturdy prentice boys from Assisi responded with the most bruising phrases in their vocabulary. Phrases led to blows, blows often to cuts and slashes.

It needed only a spark to set the dry tinder ablaze. The spark was tossed by a certain Girardo di Ghislerio, lord of Sassorosso, possessor of lands on the Assisan side of the border between the two cities. He put himself under the protection of Perugia, which then demanded that Assisi rebuild his ruined castle. On Assisi's inevitable refusal Girardo renounced his Assisan citizenship and claimed that of Perugia. In January 1200 the Perugian consuls accepted him into their fellowship and formally claimed his lands from Assisi.

This was a more than adequate *casus belli*. Everyone prepared for the conflict, though with deliberation. Some of the Assisan nobles defected to Perugia. Others made a fine show of fidelity, and raised a troop of noble cavalry. Francis of course volunteered. He busied himself finding a battle-trained mount, scarce and dear, and preparing his equipment, probably a long coat of mail, a helmet, a long, straight sword, and a ten-foot lance. He must have cut a fine figure, but he must have found his armament confoundedly heavy on his small hands and delicate fingers. His mettlesome charger was hard to manage. Full armor was brutally expensive, especially a coat of mail with its thousands of links hand-hammered into place. His father paid the bills — with protesting pride, we may suppose.

We may suppose further that Francis was happy to be accepted in the cavalry troop, for a mounted man has always looked down on the footslogger, and the cavalry has always been, to our own mechanic days, the noble arm. But one suspects that pain mingled with his joy. His companions were mostly young nobles, stalwart and muscular, created by the natural selection of the Germanic feudal lords. They were trained from babyhood as predators' cubs, in hunting, swordplay, jousting. Francis, physically at a disadvantage and educated to cloth-cutting and accounting, must have suffered from their horseplay.

At first the Perugian war was not very serious. It consisted of raids, ambushes of merchants, crop destruction, seizure of hostages, as in any guerrilla war, but done with an Italian flourish, manifested by the black *vessillo del guasto,* flag of destruction, carried by raiders bent on devastation.

In November 1202 Assisi finally declared itself ready for battle. The army was divided into units from different parishes and from various trades — the merchants, the shoemakers, the butchers. It does not sound like an efficient order of battle. The troops were followed by the *carroccio,* a cart covered with banners of the city's colors, red and blue, and drawn by four or six of the noble white oxen that still sway in step along Umbrian roads. It was something like the Hebrew Ark of the Covenant; but its stately progress must have slowed the army's march. Banners waved, trumpets and drums resounded, men shouted and sang. Any military man would have been shocked by such to-do, for certainly Perugia had its intelligence agents out, ready to report enemy movements.

The army marched directly west some ten miles to the River Tiber, the boundary between Assisan and Perugian territory. The expeditionaries seized a castle and a leper hospital, both on the Assisan side. By this time the Perugians, well warned, had occupied the river crossings. The Assisans, tired from their march, were nevertheless filled with ardor. The archers and crossbowmen discharged their shafts, the cavalry plunged in the stream and struggled across and up again, to engage in hand-to-hand combat. There was much hot work, we are told. However, it ended quickly with the victory of Perugia, which must have had an overwhelming superiority of numbers, as of terrain. Many of the Assisan knightly cavalrymen were captured. Among them was Francis.

This was his only experience of warfare. He was bold, we are assured, *non modicum audax*. Indeed, he was probably foolhardly in his effort to impress and outdo his noble companions. Lacking combat training, he was certainly incompetent. In any case, his dreams of glory were suddenly and summarily dashed.

Because of his fine manners, and perhaps because of the reputation of his wealthy father, he was imprisoned with the noble captives. The narratives picture the usual horrors — darkness, cold, massive chains. Some of the horrors may have been literary conventions, for the gentlemen prisoners seem to have had a good deal of freedom. Francis was distinguished by his cheerfulness and high spirits. When the others reproached him for his untimely cheer, he made an astonishing reply: "Certainly I am joyful; and why? I have something you don't realize in my mind.

I rejoice because one day I shall be venerated throughout the whole world!"

What can we make of that statement? Is it perhaps a myth, attributed to the speaker by a later writer with a knowledge of later events and a desire to provide a prophecy for his saint? Hardly; our authority is Tommaso da Celano, contemporary with Francis, and a usually scrupulous reporter. The words were either inspiration or the product of prodigious vanity. Certainly they were received with loud laughter in the Perugian jail. But no one is likely to laugh at them today.

By the end of the year (1203) he was released, to pursue his destiny. He may have been ill; he may very likely have been ransomed by his father. It is equally likely that the Perugians did not regard him as a very dangerous enemy.

A year's captivity had worked upon his spirit. He was now twenty-one, fully a man. He had seen men die in battle and amid the privations of prison life. And he had seen the noble companions whom he had so admired turn mean and base in confinement. He found them empty in mind, empty of high purpose.

He was welcomed back triumphantly by the Company of Tripudiantes and by Brunetta, Letizia, Colata, and the rest. Once more he was acclaimed Master of the Dance and was permitted to designate himself to pay the bills. But he could not pick up the old life where he had let it fall. In prison he had thought too much, grown too much. The old amusements were insipid. A fit of depression would seize him in the midst of the feast, and that still, small voice that harries the young would ask: "Is this all? Is this what I am here for?"

The combined reminiscences of the Three Companions

of Francis tell how, as host, he prepared a magnificent feast. Afterwards the company went singing through the town, while Francis, with his wand of office, marched in the rear.

Suddenly he received a visit from our Lord. So marvelous a sweetness filled his heart that he could neither speak nor move; he could feel nothing but this sweetness, which had rendered him immune to physical sensation. He declared later that if one had essayed to cut him in pieces he could not have made a move to escape. His companions, astonished, asked: "What were you thinking of, to abandon us? Were you perhaps thinking of taking a wife?" "Yes," he said. "I was thinking of getting engaged, to the most noble, rich, and beautiful fiancée you have ever seen." They laughed at him. He had not however spoken of his own volition, but under God's inspiration. For in fact his fiancée was the actual life of religion, which poverty renders more noble, rich, and beautiful than all others.

This is the first recorded example of Francis's mystical experiences, of his communication with the divine. He was filled with disgust of the world and with longing for the life of religion. This is the first stage of the well-trodden Mystic Way, the stage of awakening or conversion. He could, of course, have followed in the steps of the innumerable Christian mystics who had sought spiritual joy in monastic life. But he recoiled from making a profession in one of the established orders. Profoundly original, he was developing a private technique of ecstatic possession. He had to define the life of religion in his own terms.

He withdrew from the frolicsome club, and went into

a kind of retreat within the world. His mood of question-
ing and gloom was aggravated by illness, a constant low
fever, probably contracted in prison. For a time he was
put to bed; then he stumbled about the house, supported
by a cane. He ventured out to contemplate the beauty
of the world, and found he could not invest it with the
old magic. When he recovered health, with the spring of
1204, he returned no doubt to his duties in the shop, and
no doubt also to his old boredom and sense of futility,
from which he found solace in dreams of glory.

There was at this time, that is, in 1204 and 1205, a
French Count Gautier de Brienne, who had set up a
kingdom in the territory of Lecce, in Apulia, papal territory in the heel of Italy. Possessing tastes already a little
antiquarian, he formed there a chivalrous court, complete
with knights-errant, troubadours, jousts and amorous
hunting parties and music and dance and attacks on enchanted castles defended by beautiful ladies using roses
for missiles. There was plenty of actual fighting, too, with
the capture of cities to add to the pope's dominions. An
unnamed youth in Assisi proposed to Francis that the two
should join the band of brilliant knights in Lecce, where
they would dazzle all by their prowess, gaining glory and
the smiles — at the very least, the smiles — of the beautiful ladies. The fact that Francis had never been dubbed a
knight did not deter him. Regardless of the languishing
war with Perugia, all too ugly and sordid, Francis prepared for knight-errantry. He assembled a fine court costume out of stock, and bought suitable weapons and
armor. We are assured by the chroniclers that he cut a
very fine figure.

But, trying out his equipment on a country ride, he
chanced to meet a noble friend reduced to penury by the

wars. The ragged noble cast obviously envious glances at Francis's magnificence. Moved by impulse, Francis stripped himself of his glittering finery and bestowed all on the gentleman, who accepted it with no recorded hesitation. The commentators see in Francis's act a conscious imitation of Saint Martin dividing his robe with a beggar. I doubt if the act was an imitation. More likely it was prompted by shame that he, an unfit warrior, still rickety with illness, should go gloriously accoutered while the professional soldier, ruined in the wars, should be so outshone. Or let us say that his deed sprang simply from the urge of charity, which is a reality needing no precedent or interpretation.

That night he had a vivid dream. He saw all the rooms of his home packed and piled with weapons, armor, and battle harness. And he heard a voice proclaiming: "These arms are for you and your knights!" In the morning he arose joyful, confident that the Lord promised him fame and glory in the faraway court of Gautier de Brienne. He did not recognize that the surface interpretation of a dream is bound to be false.

Many asked him why he was so gay. He replied: "I know that I shall become a great prince!" He was quite right. He was to be a great prince indeed; but he could not foresee what would be the prince's rule and dominion.

He quickly assembled a makeshift equipage for a knight, and, with his noble companion, set forth on the road which would lead them through Spoleto, Rome, and Naples to Apulia. On the way his nightly fevers resumed, and his friend, impatient, pushed on, giving him a rendezvous at Lecce. To recuperate, Francis stopped at Spoleto, a friendly city. As it turned out, it was just as well that he was balked of his purpose. During his illness in Spoleto, the paragon of chivalry he wished to join, Gautier de Brienne, was killed in battle, and his quaint court soon fell to pieces.

Say the Three Companions:

> One day he had drowsed off, when he heard a voice asking whither he wished to go. Willingly he laid bare all his purpose. Then said the voice: "Who can profit you most, the master or the servant?" "The master," he replied. "Then why are you quitting the master for the servant, the prince for the subject?" Then Francis put the question: "Lord, what would you have me do?" "Return to your homeland," said the voice, "and there you will be told what you have to do, for you must understand in a quite new way the vision you have had in dream."

He roused from his torpor, and reflected long on the meaning of his dream. In the morning he took again the road to Assisi. He returned home humiliated, half sick, penniless, to be greeted with the reproaches of his father and the jesting, double-edged congratulations of his jolly companions. His effort for knightly distinction had ended in a merely ridiculous charity, gleefully retold among the great.

Thus for the second time Francis's ambitions for worldly glory collapsed in contact with reality. For the second time the knight was defeated and shamed. He was twenty-four years old and a failure in everything he had undertaken. He knew himself to be sickly, incompetent, the butt of his family, the dupe of his sycophantic friends. Unknowing, he had entered on the second stage of the Mystic Way, the stage of purgation. He had been singled out for revelation, not by a blinding bolt from heaven, as in the case of Saint Paul, but by long, painful meditation, self-torture, as in the case of Saint Augustine. Whatever the world might do or say, Francis knew that God had chosen him and would henceforth guide him.

THREE

"Repair My House"

IN THAT MIDDLE AGE the Church occupied men's life and thought in a way now unexampled in Christian countries. Proportionately to population, the clergy numbered about ten times as many as today. Half the men one met on the street were clerics of one sort or another, though distinguished chiefly by the tonsure. The clerical uniform was not yet generally imposed. Pope Innocent III ruled that the clergy must wear black, though the somber exterior was no proof of inward virtue. Most men entered the Church only for advantage, for access to jobs. Acceptance of the minor orders — acolyte, reader, doorkeeper, and the rest — did not debar one from marriage or from fleshly indulgence. The Church was omnipresent. It held entire control over education; every teacher, every university student was a tonsured clerk. As such, he escaped from civil justice, capricious and cruel, and by "benefit of clergy" had his misdeeds tried in the Church court, likely to be understanding and merciful to its own. The Church courts had jurisdiction over all cases involv-

ing marriage, contracts under oath, wills and inheritances.
The Church ran the hospitals, administered poor relief,
lodged pilgrims and impecunious travelers; indeed, it
performed most of the social functions of the modern
state.

By any statistical reckoning, the Church reached its
summit of power, wealth, and prestige in these early years
of the thirteenth century. But its material success was
not matched by spiritual fervor. The vast, miscellaneous
membership of the clergy included many, perhaps most,
whose faith was less than lukewarm, whose moral behavior
more than dubious. The lower clergy reflected the spirit
of the upper hierarchy. A bad pope, a succession of bad
popes, provoked a lowered morale among the clerics and
cynicism or even rebellion among the laity. A good pope
could by his own spiritual power recharge the entire
gigantic machine of the Church.

Innocent III was a good pope, indeed, one of the great
popes. A Roman noble, relative of high prelates, he entered the Church as a matter of course and promptly rose
to be cardinal, although merely a deacon. The historian
Albert Hauck sums him up as "a man of this world, a
man of great gifts, of sharp intelligence and unbending
will, but also of strong individuality. Also, his friends have
not denied that he could not endure opposition; he was
violent and quick to anger." He was fiercely ambitious,
for himself and for the Church, and perfectly courageous
and confident. But he was unloved, unlovable; he was a
sour ascetic, who lived largely on lemons.

The papal throne fell vacant in 1198, and Innocent,
aged only thirty-seven, was elected by his brother cardinals to fill it. He received the priesthood with unprece-
dented speed. He reigned until 1216, and in these years

papal dominance reached its zenith. Innocent's authority was recognized throughout Europe. He thought nothing of excommunicating half the kings of Christendom. The German emperor was humbled, England and Aragon became papal fiefs, the king of France was subservient. Was this enough? Did Innocent desire, and attempt, to rule the world? Historians still argue the case, but it did not concern our Francis, nor need it concern us.

Successful as Innocent was in his external policy, he could do little to cleanse the inward state of the Church. At the higher levels, simony was rife. "It is a running sore," wrote Innocent, "to be corrected only by fire and sword." Buyers of office expected to make the most of their incumbency before selling out to the highest bidder. Corruption was almost universal. John of Salisbury, a little before our time, to be sure, said: "In the Roman Church there inheres a certain root of duplicity and stimulant of avarice which is the source and root of all evils." Later writers bear him out. Francis's Three Companions allege that before his advent the love and fear of God were almost extinct, that penitence was hardly known — indeed, it was regarded as folly. "The pleasures of the flesh, lust for wealth, and pride of life so reigned that the whole world seemed to be in their grip."

The parish priests, having obtained their livings by purchase or favor, were more concerned with the collection of tithes than with the administration of sacraments. Marriage of priests and deacons was formally forbidden, but the bishops possessed and widely exercised the right of *collagium,* by which clerics were permitted to keep concubines for a fee. (Remember the priest's haughty wife in Chaucer.) The monks in their monasteries generally avoided the grosser sins in their pursuit of salvation. Their temptations were of another sort, in the administration of their enormous properties in land and goods. Said Roland Bainton: "The monastic orders were forever being undone by their virtues, which created wealth that in turn corrupted virtue."

With cynicism in high place and torpor in low the faith was bound to suffer. Instead of inspiring its professors to spiritual adventure, faith became a routine of acts and formulas, a fetichism of amulets and relics, a means of dodging God's just punishments by purchasing immunities from unworthy priests. And to those who protested the priest's unworthiness, answer was made that the efficacy of the sacraments was not affected by the worth or unworth of the ministers. Francis himself made the point in later years. A heretic, a Patarene, tried to trap him, asserting that the local priest notoriously kept a concubine. Said the heretic: "Tell me, if a priest keeps a concubine and thus soils his hands, must we accept his teaching and show respect for the sacraments he administers?" Francis went to kneel before the priest, and said: "I don't know if those hands of yours are soiled, as the man says. What I do know is this: even if they were soiled, that would not diminish the virtue and efficacy of God's sacraments. Those hands are the channel through which flow the graces and benefits of God upon the people." On his knees, he kissed the priest's soiled hands.

Many — the idealists, the naturally pious, and the natural troublemakers — called for reform of the Church, the establishment. The forthstanding leaders of protest were called heretics, and many were burned for their opinions. But if the protesting movements gained sufficiently wide acceptance, their ideas became orthodox, their programs salutary reforms, their leaders saints.

All the heretical groups called for a purification of the Church, not a rejection of it. They represented the virtuous poor, shocked by the idleness and vice of the rich. In this sense the heresies were proletarian movements, social as well as doctrinal, and they were dangerous to the ruling class. Hence, no doubt, the ferocity of the repression of the Albigensians in France, known in Italy as the Cathari, or Patarenes (after the *pataria,* the flea market of Milan). We need not examine the doctrines of the Patarenes, the Amauricians, the Waldensians, and others. Enough that Francis's movement was one of several. It could easily have been declared heretical and have gone underground. But Francis would not argue about doctrine. He was simply not interested in theology; he was bored by it and by theologians. For him faith came from the heart, not from the intellect, which is by its nature fallible.

Francis was experimenting with himself, and with God's will as well. In the spring of 1206, when folk long to go on pilgrimages, he joined a pilgrim band bound for Rome. (Or was it in 1205, and must all the dates on the next few pages be set back a year? Those who may wish to examine the very confusing, and confused, arguments should consult the appendix to Omer Englebert's *Saint Francis of Assisi.**)

Always careful to dress the part, Francis donned a coarse gown and carried a long staff. At Saint Peter's, the predecessor of the present basilica, he made the rounds of prayer and offering, but received no personal message. He stopped at a grated window above the tomb of Saint Peter; through the window the pilgrims were tossing coins, to ring on the bronze floor below, as in a

* Chicago, Franciscan Herald Press, 1965.

holy cash register. It seemed to Francis that his fellows
were tossing few coins, and those of the smallest denomi-
nation. With one of his magnificent gestures he pulled
out his traveling money and threw most of it down with
a notable crash. The act was generous indeed, though it
does bear a look of Pharisaic ostentation.

The forecourt of Saint Peter's was the gathering place
of all the beggars of Rome, a swarming mass of human
horrors. Francis called to one of them and arranged to
change clothes for the day. He begged, in French — it is
not clear just why, unless he felt that the French was
part of a disguise, a game. Anyway, people who know
French are almost certain to show it off, à tort et à travers.
At the day's end Francis joined his friend the professional
beggar and supped with him at a table set out in honor
of the day, the Feast of the Holy Martyrs, 13 May. He
and the beggar then resumed their proper clothes. His
experience is said to be "a great victory, the triumph of
compassion over natural pride." Or perhaps it could be
regarded as the triumph of curiosity over natural squeam-
ishness, a testing of poverty by playing beggar, without
commitment.

Francis returned to Assisi, to his melancholy life of
self-examination and self-accusation. Apparently his
father had abandoned all hope of making a businessman
of him, and life at home was intolerable, with an angry
father, a reproachful mother, and a scornful brother. He
was treated as the household idiot. He devoted himself to
almsgiving, presenting money, food, or clothes to any
asker. The substance of his alms must have come from
petty thievery in the home. He would load the family
table with food, to augment the leavings for the poor.
But to give away one's leavings is not so very meritorious.

"A bone to the dog is not charity," said someone — it could have been Francis.

His discord with his father became open warfare. "His father loved him much," say the Three Companions. But father and son could not meet without tempers flaring, even without paternal curses. Francis invented a typical equivocation to turn aside the consequences of curses. He adopted a wretched beggar as his father, saying: "When you see my father curse me, I will say: 'Father, give me your blessing.' Then you will make the sign of the cross upon me, and you will bless me in his stead." This soft answer, far from turning away wrath, merely increased it — as must have been foreseen.

Francis took to solitary wandering, seeking out places where he could be alone and secure. One day he was riding his horse — or the dry-goods business horse — in the country. He passed near the leper hospital, operated by a group of holy, devoted churchmen. Francis had a particular horror of the lepers, who were then numerous. He alleged that he could smell one two miles off, and would stop his nose against their infection. But on this day he encountered a leper who stood in the very roadway, against all the rules. He clapped heels to horse, and rode on; then, suddenly engulfed in shame, he returned, dismounted, and kissed the astonished leper on his dribbling mouth. Or was he astonished, even capable of astonishment? According to one account, when Francis looked back the leper had vanished into air.

Another day Francis discovered a perfect refuge for his torturing thoughts. It was a tiny church, or chapel, a mile from Assisi, dedicated to Saint Damian, that wonder-working physician. Its setting was unkempt, weed-grown, its roof leaky, its floor filthy. But it was not totally aban-

doned. Over the smutted altar hung a fine life-size cruci-
fix, in Byzantine style. The Christ was strangely moving,
alive, with great melancholy eyes. (And he still lives, the
wonder of Saint Clare's convent church in Assisi.)

As Francis knelt in prayer, the wide-open eyes of the
Savior were fixed upon him. The lips moved and spoke:
"Francis, go and repair my house, which, as you see, is
falling all to ruin." Twice more the words were repeated.
The lips closed and were still; the command faded from
the black Byzantine eyes. But their illumination remained in Francis's heart — the illumination that lights
the third stage of the Mystic Way.

The words "repair my house" fell on welcoming ears.
The literal meaning was clear enough. But for the figura-
tive, the greater meaning — did Francis apprehend it immediately, or only later?

He sought out the priest, named Pietro, in formal charge
of the edifice. Pietro shrugged his shoulders. There was
nothing to be done. There was no congregation, no willing hands to rebuild and restore, and above all no
money. Why bother? There were plenty of churches — too
many. Better have fewer and more prosperous churches.

The reluctance of the priest to believe, or to heed,
Christ's command roused the combative spirit in Francis
and turned him from melancholy dreamer to man of action, though highly imprudent action in the world's
view. He visited the family shop, made a bundle of the
finest materials in stock, especially the brilliant, much-
prized scarlet, loaded them on the delivery horse, and,
since obviously he could make no sales in Assisi, trotted
off to Foligno, a dozen miles away. In that market he sold
his cloth and also the horse. Jingling his pocketful of gold,
he walked back to San Damiano. "A present for San

Damiano!" he cried, displaying his treasure to the priest Pietro. But the timid cleric was shocked and apprehensive of trouble; he refused to accept the dangerous gift. No one could outdo Francis in scorn of money; he tossed his hoard into the embrasure of a window. The window, *la finestra del denaro,* is still to be seen at Saint Damian's. (But the gold has gone.)

When Pietro Bernardone heard the news, he fell into what was probably the greatest rage of his life. The boy was not only mad, he was a thief, a criminal! To restore some crazy country chapel he would ruin his father, his mother, his brother! He was a menace to society! He must be stopped!

Francis prudently left his home and took up lodging in Saint Damian's. There he found a niche, still to be seen, where he is said to have hidden from his father. Even more prudently, he enrolled himself as an oblate, or cleric-in-training, with the priest of Saint Damian's, thus qualifying for certain clerical privileges, such as the right of sanctuary. Apparently he was amazed at the reception given his exploit. He had expected to be acclaimed for his generosity; instead he was avoided by his former friends and abused by the masses. Boys followed him in the street, shouting "Get the crazy man!" and pelting him with stones and muck. The fact is that even the mob, the proletariat, regarded his act as subversive of commercial morality and respect for parents and the family, indeed, subversive of all society. If property is not safe, there is no safety. Even the propertyless will defend this proposition.

For a time Pietro let his son go his own way. But one day he heard in the street near his house a great howling and hooting. He looked out to see a crowd of boys and men pursuing his son. This was a cruel blow to his pride. He took Francis in and confined him in the cellar. And when called away on business he summoned a smith to rivet chains on the young man's legs. But during his absence his wife had the chains filed off, and set Francis free to go where he would.*

Pietro returned from his business trip to find his son gone and his wife in rebellion. Francis had retreated no farther than Saint Damian's. There the father sought him out. The interview may have begun calmly, but it ended in furious mutual defiance. Francis abjured his natural father, and declared he had no true parent but God. Pietro's answer was inevitable: "You can tell that to the judge!" He had an excellent case against his son, who had robbed him of valuable goods and a horse and had rebelled against parental authority. The statutes of Assisi provided that such offenses were punishable by banishment from the city and deprivation of the rights of inheritance within the family, and all citizens were forbidden to give the culprit food, drink, or succor.

Pietro presented his complaint to the city's rulers. Francis pled lack of jurisdiction on the part of the civil court; as a servant of the Most High he was exempt from human justice. The civil authorities countered by arranging his ecclesiastical trial before the bishop of

* This story inspires much mistrust in the present writer. It sounds like all the tales of shacked victims in dungeons, part of the melodrama of medieval life. There are difficulties. Customers in the shop would have been disagreeably impressed by screams and yells from the cellar. How did that smith forge the shackles? Did he transport his forge and anvil to the Bernardone shop? Or was Francis paraded through the streets to the smithy? Either procedure would have caused excited talk. Too many people are involved in the story. Further, Pietro Bernardone, as I see him, would not have been so crude. He loved his son, in his own way. He might have locked him in; but keeping him in irons is out of character.

Assisi, in the portico of the Church of Santa Maria Maggiore. This was a break for the accused, for Bishop Guido was a battler for the Church's rights who evidently liked Francis and had no love for his father.

Those involved met on a bitterly cold afternoon in January 1207 (or was it 1206?). There followed one of the most dramatic episodes in legal history. One may see the background and the climax of the drama in Giotto's famous fresco in the Upper Church at Assisi. Bishop Guido and his staff, well muffled in their heavy furred robes, emerged from the church door; Pietro Bernardone, with a considerable party of friends and bystanders, confronted them. The bishop ordered Francis to stand forth. Pietro Bernardone detailed his grievances. Francis admitted the charges, making only the defense that he was fulfilling the injunctions of a higher law. The bishop reminded Francis that ill-gotten gains bring only ill, and commanded him to return to his father the money received for the sale of the cloth and the horse. To the crowd Francis proclaimed: "Now I am quits, and free! I can freely say: 'Our Father who art in heaven!' Pietro Bernardone is no longer my father! I return to him not only my money — here it is — but also all my clothes. I shall go naked to meet my naked Lord!" Therewith he stripped off all his clothes — though some authorities mention a hair shirt — and tossed them, with a purse of money, to his confounded father. The bishop, for decency's sake, stepped down from his throne, flung off his rich cloak and wrapped it around the shivering figure. He acted, no doubt, from impulse, but by his deed he made a symbolic promise to put Francis under the Church's protection. A quick-witted cleric ran up with the blouse of a farm laborer. This Francis marked with a cross, "thus making it meet for a man crucified, poor and half naked."

Francis's gesture was superbly dramatic, as a means of shaming his father with ridicule. Take someone by surprise by tossing to him a bag of money and a bundle of clothing; he cannot resist catching and holding them, though awkwardly. Least of all could a cloth merchant bear to see fine materials trampled in dirty snow. Humiliated, Pietro Bernardone turned homeward, clutching his sorry possessions. The bystanders, whose sympathy had been caught by Francis's drama of self-stripping, pursued the father with mocks and hoots.

The mocks and hoots of writers and readers still pursue Pietro Bernardone down the frozen street of time. Few show him any Christian charity. I grieve for him, as Francis never did. The father had merely followed the businessman's ethic of his class and time. There may be loftier ethics, but the businessman's ethic is at least an ethic, and Pietro Bernardone was never accused of violating it or of lacking probity and honor. He had educated his son with affectionate, perhaps foolish, liberality, had indulged his slightest whim, had, according to direct testimony, loved him, and had been rewarded only with scorn and hate. He was simply bewildered; why was he to be howled down for trying to save his family's property from ruin?

And what of Francis's mother? We are told, on rather insecure authority, that Francis never entered the family home after his trial. If he ever saw his mother again, it must have been in chance encounters in the city streets. Despite the scriptural command to disciples, this seems harsh treatment on the part of a saint, the great preacher of love.

Francis spent the rest of the winter praying, practicing begging, and desultorily restoring Saint Damian's chapel. At the first coming of spring the old ferment worked in his blood. He took to the roads again, not, apparently, making a pilgrimage but taking a walking tour in the hills to the north, toward Gubbio. "He entered a forest," says Tommaso da Celano, "singing God's praises in French." (No doubt singing in French betokened a joyful heart.) "Suddenly some brigands leaped out at him and asked him in a threatening manner who he was. 'I am the herald of the Great King; do you mind?' replied the man of God, firmly and composedly." But the robbers were proof against Francis's charm and whimsical fancies, and even robbers hate to be mocked. "They manhandled him, stripped him of his tunic, and threw him into a deep ditch full of snow, saying: 'Lie there, damned herald of God!' When they were well away, Francis struggled with hands and feet to free himself from the snow, climbed out of the ditch, laughed heartily, and made the woods ring ever louder with praise of the Creator of all things."

His gaiety soon faded, as the cold winds of reality bit into his barely covered flesh, as hunger sharpened the cold. The best of French songs could not avail to stifle his misery. He came then to a Benedictine monastery, probably that of Valfabbrica, seven or eight miles from Assisi. When he asked for food and lodging, he was given a coarse gown and put to work as a scullion. He was granted a single blanket and a heel of moldy bread, which he was forbidden even to dip in the stew pot reserved for the monastic pigs. He would gladly have pushed on, but the melting snows flooded the countryside.

Perhaps the stay in the monks' kitchen was a test set by

Lady Poverty, revealing the truth of her condition. Her grim favors, which all the world flees, are to be gained only by self-stripping, by humility.

Humility is a virtue little practiced in our modern world. We are likely to deny it altogether, as a conscious deception, as practiced by Uriah Heep, or as a hidden arrogance presenting a lack as a merit. Humility, we say, is a disorder of the human spirit; all humility is false humility. Psychology has devalued it, together with virtue and sin. When the searcher for perfection thinks he has attained humility, he has merely gained pride under a false name. Says the contemporary *Mirror of Perfection:* "In [Francis's] thought and desire, self-abasement was bound to be a very great elevation in the eyes of God and men." Well then, if self-abasement becomes elevation in the eyes of God and men it is no longer self-abasement. It is demonic self-glorification; it is pride.

The waters abated; Francis took again to the roads. He climbed the windy ridge to the north and descended to Gubbio, that austere but lovely city, ancient in an ancient world. There he found in a monastery an old friend, who took him in and fed and clothed him. When restored, he turned about and took the homeward way to Assisi.

He reached some profitable conclusions on his long walk. He realized that he must humble his lurking pride, find salvation in the rejection of all his desires for comfort and ease. He must embrace the misery and evil of the world. And since the lepers were the most repulsive manifestation of misery and evil, he must embrace the lepers. He presented himself at the lazar house near Assisi and offered his services. He washed the outcasts' rotting feet, bandaged their open sores, stanched and even kissed their horrid wounds. All this self-disciplining was "for the love of God," we are told, not, it seems, for the love of man, the love of lepers.

Francis, examining his spirit, concluded that he must cease balancing between the civil world of Assisi and the spiritual world. He said in his Testament: "When I was still in sin, the mere sight of lepers was unbearable to me. But the Lord himself brought me among them and I tended them with all good will. By the time I left them, what had seemed to me so ugly had turned into sweetness in body and mind. So I waited a little while, and then said farewell to the world."

However, he did not actually bid farewell to the world, only to the revolting service of the lepers. If he had really wished to leave the world, he could have taken the way chosen by so many other pious, troubled young men, who joined monastic orders to live lives of total devotion in total obscurity. But Francis was shocked by the uncharitableness and the material preoccupations of the Benedictines of Valfabbrica. And he was no joiner; he hated rules and subjections. He demanded freedom, to work, pray, sing, at his own times and at his own direction. He declared himself ready to submit absolutely to the Lord's will; but on his own terms. He would set the terms.

FOUR

The Espousal of Lady Poverty

As Francis had shut the doors of his home against himself, he found lodging in the crazy chapel of Saint Damian. The enormous suffering Christ above the altar reminded his guest, reproachfully, of the words He had spoken in vision — "Repair my house." Francis took them in the literal sense, and repaired walls and patched gaps when he felt in the mood. He did the same for another abandoned chapel, San Pietro della Spina, which has now relapsed to become a *contadino*'s barn. And he found, in the *selva grossa,* a dreary, marshy woodland about two miles from the city, another tiny chapel crying for help. There stood nearby a large thatched cabin which could serve as a meetingplace, and some crude wattle-and-daub huts. The chapel was called the Portiuncula, the Little Portion, or the Small Holding. The roof was partly gone; the sacred furniture flaunted its desolation and neglect. Only, in the sanctuary, the image of the Virgin persisted. Now the great modern church of Santa Maria degli Angeli has been built around it, to contain within, before its altar, the tiny chapel of the Portiuncula, shining and bejeweled. It is the bourn of innumerable pilgrims who come there to seek indulgences for their sins.*

The Portiuncula was a dependency of the Benedictines of Monte Subasio, who on high days sent a priest there to say mass and collect candle money. On Saint Matthias's Day, 24 February 1209 (or else 1208), Francis was one of the few worshipers. The celebrant read the Gospel, Matthew X, Christ's instructions to his apostles: "Heal the sick, raise the dead, cleanse lepers, cast out demons. . . . Take no gold, nor silver, nor copper in your belts, no bag for your journey, nor two tunics, nor sandals, nor a staff."† The words, he knew, were addressed to him. With the literalness of the unlettered, he cast away his shoes (it was February, remember), his purse and his staff. He kept only his tunic and replaced his belt by the triply knotted rope that every Franciscan wears. The course of his life was now determined by direct communication from the divine.

In Assisi he became a familiar eccentric. He visited the churches and chapels, carrying a broom to sweep out the numerous dirty corners and littered recesses. He wore a patched, ragged gown, out of humility, he thought, but Pietro Bernardone's son in rags made a sensation in the city streets. He could have found no better way to attract attention. He lived by begging, and developed a technique of demanding proudly, peremptorily. For, he said, the asking of alms for the love of God is an act of

---

* And in California, matching San Francesco's city, stands another city of three million souls, bearing formally the name of "El Pueblo de Nuestra Señora la Reina de los Ángeles de Porziuncola." How far that little candle throws its beams!

† The phrasing is from the Revised Standard Version, Catholic edition.

the utmost nobility, dignity, and courtesy before God;
the beggar offers God's love in payment. Alms are the
right of the poor. At the same time the almsgiver cleanses
his soul of spots of sin. The shame lies on him who re-
fuses to give, not on him who asks. But Francis received
many harsh words and sour looks in his quest for alms.
People said: "He threw away his own property and now
he comes and begs for ours!"

Gradually, however, repulsion yielded to curiosity, and
curiosity to respect. Francis's rejection of social dogmas
and sanctions touched a response in many hearts; it answered men's so-frequent longing to cast off the useless
baggage of existence and return to the essential simplicity
of the self. The symbol of his new life was stripping,
physical and mental. He sought rejection, deprivation,
fasting, nothingness, the void. Therein he found joy.
The world saw Francis's gaiety of spirit, and envied him,
not realizing the refusals that underlay it. Men began to
seek him out, and to tell him of their sympathy, their
envy.

The first recruit was an anonymous Assisan, who
dropped away when his courage failed him. The second
was of different mettle. He was Bernardo di Quintavalle,
one of the *majores* of the city, a noble, a scholar with a
doctorate in civil and canon law from Bologna, a man of
wealth and standing. Of course he and Francis were
acquainted, from the days of their wanton youth. Some
canker was working within him, some welling disgust.
One evening in April 1209, a month when nature makes
her greatest transformations, Bernardo met Francis by
chance and asked him to dine in his palazzo. (It still
stands, though much altered.) The candles were spent
before the young men's talk was done. Bernardo had a

second bed prepared beside his own; and all night long he heard Francis crying: "My God! My God!" in an agony of prayer. In the morning he told Francis that he had made up his mind to join him, abandoning the world.

"Let us seek the counsel of our Lord Jesus Christ!" said Francis. The two repaired to the nearest church, prayed and heard mass, and asked the priest to open the Gospels at random and put his finger on a verse, which might, by God's grace, prove to be a message. So it was; the words under the priest's finger were: "If you would be perfect, go, sell what you possess and give to the poor, and you will have treasure in heaven: and come, follow me." They made a second trial, and found the words: "Take nothing for your journey, no staff, nor bag, nor bread, nor money; and do not have two tunics." And on a third trial: "If any man would come after me, let him deny himself, and take up his cross and follow me."

Thereupon Bernardo set about selling his possessions, and distributed all to the poor, widows, orphans, pilgrims, monasteries and hospitals. Like a modern foundation, he gave to the deserving poor, rather than to those who were merely hungry, probably through their own fault.

In the event Bernardo developed a gift for voluntary trance. He could stand rapt and insensible in church from dawn to noon. He lived for weeks on solitary mountaintops, his mind, in contemplation of divinity, soaring like the swallows.

Bernardo set the precedent for men who were troubled and desirous, but timid. He brought in his friend Pietro di Catanio, gentleman and doctor of laws. There was Brother Egidio (or Gilio, or Giles), stout and hearty, as loud in jest as in prayer. He said that his state was like that of a newlywed, who wants to adorn his bride with finery, but when the hour of love comes he discards everything for naked union. "Thus good works adorn the soul, but truth unites the partners." Again, when he preached against incontinence, an auditor protested: "This doesn't apply to me; I am married, and I don't go cheating my wife." "Can't a man get drunk on wine from his own barrel?" asked Egidio. And remember his splendid epigram: "The Bible is God talking baby-talk."

Then there was Angelo Tancredi, a noble knight and a special favorite of Francis. Commoners enlisted, too, for there could be no aristocracy of souls. Very dear to Il Poverello — the Little Poor Man, as he began to be called — was Brother Leo, ordained a priest in time to become his master's confessor as well as his secretary. He was pure and innocent as a dove, indeed more so than most doves. Francis called him Frate Pecorella, or Pecorone, because he had a large head like a sheep. And Elias, later director of the order, already foretokening his abilities as a big executive. One day Francis noticed him wearing a gown of fine material, which, as an old cloth dealer, he recognized. He borrowed the gown, put it on, and paraded before the brothers with comic ecclesiastical majesty. "God have you in his keeping, my good people!" he intoned loftily, saying, "That is the way false brothers of our order walk." By contrast, he did an imitation of a true brother's humble, natural walk.

Then there was Brother Rufino, forever haunted by visions and rapt in ecstasies. And Brother Masseo, so tall and handsome that on begging expeditions he would collect twice as much as the master, to his annoyance. But Masseo was not very bright. Assured by Christ of divine favor, he cooed joyously and constantly like a dove: "Coo,

coo, coo!" Another brother, bored by this unchanging
note, asked why he did not vary his tune. He received the
joyful answer: "When we find full contentment in one
song there is no need to change the tune." And sweet,
comic Brother Juniper, or Ginepro, the clown of the
party. Delegated to a solemn gathering, he was found
seesawing with a couple of children. And Brother Giovanni the Simple, who imitated the master in his every
gesture and act, including coughing and spitting. And
Brother Pacifico, poet and singer, crowned King of Poets
by the emperor for his profane compositions. His task
was to lead the singing in choir. And Brother Simone, so
easily ravished aloft that when a joking companion put a
hot coal on his bare foot he did not stir till the coal had
cooled. And finally Giovanni della Cappella, John of the
Hat, who woud not be parted from his hat by any command. He left the order to found one of his own, composed of seditious lepers. But lo, the consequences! He
contracted leprosy, stole the balsam set aside to embalm
Francis's body, and finally hanged himself, to play the
part of the Franciscan Judas.

The faithful soon reached and overpassed the apostolic
count of twelve. Francis tried to stick at that holy number, for he was consciously, devoutly, practicing the Imitation of Christ. The popularity of his apostolate took
him by surprise. He had had no idea of founding an
order, with rules and by-laws, under Church authority.
He wanted to be free; having cast off all civic and social
obligations, he had no desire to assume those of the organized Church. He recognized, however, the pleasures
of presiding over a holy club, like that of the Tripudiantes, but devoted to the salvation, not the damnation, of
souls. A divine oracle gave its approval, informing him

that he might win for Christ the souls that the devil had marked for his own. And so he chose to live for all men rather than for his own pitiable self.

At first the party members were called merely the Penitents of Assisi. Then Francis invented a more appropriate name: *Frati Minori* in Italian, *Fratres Minores* in Latin, and in English Minorites or Lesser Brothers, because they must deem themselves less than all others. (They were eventually outdone by the Minims.) The name had a social connotation, for the inhabitants of Assisi were divided into two classes — the *majores,* the rulers, and the *minores,* the landless, voteless peasants and workers. The political reference was certainly in Francis's mind, but he had no class-consciousness, no rebellious purpose.

Originally there were no entrance requirements to the club, no novitiate. One merely told Francis that he wished to lead a life of evangelical perfection, and proved it by giving all his possessions to the poor.

The material problems were met by denial of their existence. Francis tried to find a home for his flock by obtaining rights to one of the musty, unused chapels that dotted the Assisan countryside. He appealed to Bishop Guido, who had befriended him against his father in the sensational stripping trial. But the bishop and his canons refused such a grant — reasonably enough, for the Church could hardly surrender its property to a crank who might, for all one knew, lapse into some horrible heresy. The Benedictines of Mount Subasio were more cordial. They ceded the little chapel of the Portiuncula to Francis for a nominal rent: an annual mess of fresh-caught carp and a pot of olive oil. Around the chapel the brothers built shaky huts of branches and clay.

Francis had already found, not far from San Damiano and the Portiuncula, a cabin by a brookside called *Rivo Torto,* Crooked Brook. Being in an area set aside as a leper colony, it was abandoned by all but a countryman's ass. This the brothers repaired and occupied, crowding miserably together, while the countryman's ass brayed in anger at his exclusion. As the Minorites grew in number, most of them moved to the Portiuncula headquarters.

At Rivo Torto and the Portiuncula the brothers huddled, sleeping on the ground and squatting to eat out of wooden bowls. They prayed and worshiped by night, and by day served the lepers and worked with the peasants in the fields. Francis was a persistent advocate of manual labor, although he does not seem to have done a great deal himself. His disciple Saint Bonaventure asserts that he achieved only about twelve deniers' worth of work in his life. He was easily bored by routine, and being bound by no obligation he could stop work whenever he pleased. However, he hated sloth, and adopted the Benedictine motto: *Ora et labora.* He said that the body, Brother Ass, must be heavily loaded, ill fed, and soundly beaten.

Brother Egidio gives us a good sample of prayer and work. He was a farm boy, ready to turn his hand to any task. He cried "water for sale" in the streets, wove baskets, and buried the dead. Having carried a backload of wood into Rome for a lady, he was offered a small tip. "My good lady," he said, "I will not let myself be overcome by avarice." But come to think of it, Brother Egidio was a wit, and the remark may have been one of his little jokes.

The brothers' possessions were kept to an absolute minimum: a gown with rope for belt, drawers or breeches, sandals in case of need. The gown was of undyed wool for cheapness's sake, and was of a nondescript gray, what the Italians call beast color. No individual towel, toothbrush, handkerchief; the brothers packed in the Rivo Torto retreat would have offended delicate nostrils. The community must have possessed cooking utensils, knives and spoons, cups or bowls. And someone owned, or kept in custody, a pair of nail scissors. The gowns were by preference ragged. Francis, with his ex-haberdasher's sense of style, outdid all in raggedness, in setting startling patches to his habit. If by chance he received an intact gown, he made the brothers contribute unnecessary patches from their own. (We have seen the proto-Franciscan style revived in our own time by youths unaware of their Franciscanism.) Francis ordered that his burial tunic be patched with sackcloth. (It is still enshrined in the Assisi basilica.) But he permitted himself a soft tunic next to the skin, so that the roughness and vileness would appear only outwardly. (This statement, from the *Mirror of Perfection*, conflicts with the assertion that in his self-stripping before the bishop he disclosed a hair shirt. Possibly; but the point of his stripping was the exhibition of total nudity.)

For food the brothers depended on charity, following the precedent of Christ and his apostles, and prefiguring the principles of modern fund-raisers. "Alms are the heritage and right of the poor," said Francis. "If one feels shame in begging, without for that reason drawing back, that shame is meritorious," he said again. He tells us that the brothers make a kind of pact with the world, giving the world the good example; the world must repay with food. And if the brothers are false to the good example, the world will cut off their food supply, and a good thing too.

The canvassers were ordered to accept only the needful, for to take more would be theft. They were not to discriminate; they put no ban on meat-eating, except on fast days. But Francis certainly discriminated, when he was invited to dine by the great Cardinal Bishop Ugolino of Ostia. Francis brought along a bag of crusts of black bread to gnaw during dinner. The cardinal was affronted, and complained that this ostentatious dieting shamed him. Francis replied: "My Lord, I have done you a great honor, since I honored a greater Lord." He emptied his crusts on the table and offered them to the other guests. Some ate, in embarrassment; others carried off the scraps as souvenirs.

Since money was taboo, food came in kind, according to the circumstances or the convenience of the almsgiver. No diet planning was possible; everything edible was served, horribly mixed, seasoned or unseasoned. The revoltingness of the messes was heightened by adherence to biblical precepts. A well-wisher contributed some dried beans. When Brother Cook put them to soak overnight, Francis stopped him, to follow the Gospel: "Take no thought for the morrow." It was easy for Francis to forego all thought for the morrow. He had little sensual liking for food. Indeed, he sometimes put water or ashes on his pittance, remarking: "Our Sister Ash is chaste." He regarded his body as something independent of himself, says Tommaso da Celano. He admitted that it is difficult to satisfy the needs of the body without yielding to the inclinations of the senses. He recognized that the new recruits, in their zeal, were inclined to overdo their austerities, wearing iron belts and hair shirts, whipping themselves with thorny branches, plunging in icy waters. He felt responsible even for the lives of his brothers, who were constantly sick, refusing medicine and doing all in their power to attract ill health. Bernardo di Quintavalle never satisfied his hunger in fifteen years; and one poor novice at Rivo Torto nearly died of starvation before being corrected and stuffed with food. Francis himself spent a Lent alone on an island in Lake Trasimeno, consuming only half a roll, and that merely to avoid vainglory in rivaling his Master. But this and other instances of his heroic fasts should be regarded with suspicion, for there are other texts to indicate his impatience with punctilious rules of behavior. These seemed to him at the very least unimportant, as they did to Christ himself.

"We should hate our bodies, with our vices and sins," he said, in a letter to the faithful. "Let us keep our bodies in humiliation and scorn, because all of us, by our own fault, are wretched, rotten, fetid." And fasting is the most obvious form of self-castigation, and the easiest. It demands of us simply that we do nothing.

But fasting is a peculiar business, a calamity but a discipline imposed by most religions. It inflicts salutary pain upon us; but it rewards the persistent with a sharpening of the senses, a mystical awareness, often an ecstatic bliss. It may be practiced by anyone, with or without hope of unearthly reward. Medical men have studied it as a mere aberration. In a carefully supervised test in 1886, a Stefano Merlatti went without food for fifty days. I read not long ago of an Englishman who for twenty years had taken no nourishment but tea with milk and sugar; he was no saint. But laymen's fasts are nothing in comparison with the refusals of holy women. Saint Catherine of Siena fasted for eight years, Blessed Angela of Foligno for twelve, with complete cessation of evacuation and urination. The recordholder is Maria Rosa Andriani (born 1790), who fasted for twenty-eight years. In a two-week medical test she was guarded by four nurses, who testified that nothing passed her lips except sacramental wafers. She lived to be seventy-two.

Prolonged fasting causes the stomach to contract like a deflated toy balloon. The digestive apparatus accustoms itself to scanty nourishment. But, we are told, in fasting the sexual impulse is by no means stilled. It may even be intensified, with the physical manifestations provoking a dreamy rapture, transforming lustful imaginations into spiritual delights. Thus fasting may lead to lewd indulgence, which can often not be quelled by more fasting. *The Little Flowers of Saint Francis* are packed with instances of diabolic temptations to carnal sin.

What is meant by carnal sin? Not, of course, sexual congress, in the circumstances of monastic life. Let us avail ourselves of the new frankness — simply erection with its accompanying fantasies, leading to voluntary or involuntary ejaculation, and ending in remorse and shame. The teaching of the Church, says the *Catholic Encyclopedia,* is that "masturbation is a serious sin that will keep one from heaven." Sleep is no refuge; the devil sends orgiastic dreams, and the unhappy friar finds in the morning evidence that he has been visited by a succuba, a masquerading fiend. The tortured spirits of the clergy were the playground of the joyful demons, where they were allowed, even commissioned, to disport themselves. "The demons are the Lord's policemen," said Francis. "They are employed in punishing the wicked. A perfect monk often sins without knowing it." Hence the devil punishes him to make him aware of his offense. A man who does not know temptation is a poor thing, Francis said again. "Harsh combats are reserved for strong souls." And God seems to blend with the old Enemy, as an encourager of sin, licensing the devil as his tempter, his *agent provocateur.*

The devil made a special effort to conquer Francis through lewd visitations, for in him evidently the fire of lust burned strong. He would doff his gown and flagellate his wicked body; he would roll in ditches full of snow, to keep his white robe of chastity undefiled, saying: "It is more tolerable for a spiritual man to bear intense cold than to feel the heat of carnal lust in his mind." Praying one night in a convent church, he was attacked by a great throng of demons; they dragged him about the church floor, while he shouted his joy in suffering. And once, pursued by the Tempter, he threw himself naked into a thorny hedge. Where his blood fell appeared a new species of thornless roses, bearing tiny red spots on their leaves. You may see the descendants of these roses, transplanted to the cloister of Santa Maria degli Angeli. They certainly have no thorns.

The best defense against the crafts and assaults of the devil is, of course, prayer. Francis's prayer was not an asking, a whining request for undeserved favors; it was a sharing with his Beloved, an intimate, spontaneous communion with Christ or his saints. As in the night of Bernardo di Quintavalle's conversion, he needed no words and uttered none, except "My God! My God!" Praying among the brethren, he avoided coughings, groanings, hard breathings and dramatic gestures. In private his dialogue with Jesus turned into a wordless rapture, an effusion of the heart rather than a muttering with the lips. He disliked the set formulas of the Church,

as he disliked all prescriptions that hampered his freedom. "Seated or walking, eating or drinking, he was
totally immersed in prayer." His state of prayer was likely
to last from evening to morning, showing itself in his face,
flaming red, and his gaping mouth. He was possessed.
"He seemed not so much a man praying as prayer itself
made man," said one who spied upon him.

He had small interest in theology and philosophy. He
and his followers were, on the whole, anti-intellectual.
He was not what we call a thinker, by which we mean, I
suppose, a systematic philosopher. He was rather a feeler,
accepting his feelings as truth, and proclaiming them in
fine, stirring phrases. He had only scorn for those "puffed
up by the wind of knowledge, *scientia inflativa*." He
said: "Brothers, you who are seduced by an excessive
desire for knowledge, you will be found emptyhanded
on the day of tribulation. Cultivate virtue. For on that
last day your books will be tossed out of the window."
He reproved those who appealed to past precedent: "God
will confound you through your wisdom and knowledge,
and I trust in the sergeants of the Lord that God will
punish you by them." Recalling, perhaps, the pridefulness
of learned clerks trying to put him to shame, he counseled
against all reading. "So many men try to climb to knowledge that he is happy who will make himself ignorant for
the love of God." A novice begged permission to have a
psalter; Francis refused him, saying: "Blessed are those
who renounce knowledge for the love of God." He added
that Christian rulers and martyrs had died for the faith;
they did not write about it. "Now many want to receive
honors and praise for merely retelling what others did.
And thus, among us, many would like to gain honors and

praise for reporting and preaching what the saints did.*
He assailed the frightened novice: "A psalter you want?
A breviary you'll be wanting next! I am the breviary! I
am the breviary!" He described circles in the air above
him, in the manner of a man washing his head. "Knowledge!" he would cry — the mere pursuit of it is hopeless.
"Your schoolbooks will do you no good. One single
demon will always be more learned than all men put together." The poor and humble, he insisted, were the best
converters, as their prayers reached the ear of God more
readily than fine-spun argument. Such pronouncements
were evidently welcome not only to the unlettered but to
disillusioned, overeducated intellectuals, such as the two
doctors of law, Bernardo di Quintavalle and Tommaso
di Catanio.

Gradually, inevitably, a kind of doctrine emerged from
Francis's antidoctrinalism. The Church was riddled with
corruption; it must be reformed. Men, tempted by the
devil and yielding to him, must be rescued, for the security of their souls. So men must be induced to lead apostolic lives, directed by the regenerated Church. Francis's
purpose was not subversive or heretical; he proposed
merely a revival of Gospel simplicity, the acceptance of
Christ's teaching and the imitation of His life.

The root of all evil lay deeper than mere love of money;
it lay in the very institution of property. Francis said to
Bishop Guido of Assisi: "From property come disputes
and lawsuits; it makes obstacles to the love of God and
one's neighbor. So we won't possess any temporal goods in
this world." One thinks of Proudhon's declaration: "Property is theft." Francis was even an ancestor of philosophical anarchism, as of so many beliefs. In practice, he came

* Ouch!

close to realizing total destitution, stopping short only of complete nakedness. Sadly enough, one always stops a little short of the absolute.

The abolition of property is a negative statement of the advocacy of poverty. Francis personified Poverty as his chosen bride. "Have you seen her whom my soul loves?" he would inquire. He was not, of course, the first to celebrate her. Not to mention the eastern ascetics, the Christian ethic produced abundant propertyless hermits, starving in caves and fastnesses. Entire orders were based on poverty — as the Humiliati and the "Poor Catholics." Some, the Poor Men of Lyons, the Waldensians, found themselves outside the Church, and were seized and burnt as heretics. But none, I think, required such a complete renunciation as did Francis, none rejected so absolutely any paltering or mitigation, none hailed Our Lady Poverty with such poetic raptures. "None was ever so greedy of gold as he of poverty," said Saint Bonaventure. He was in revulsion against all the mean subjections of his youth, against putting on the salesman's smiling face, to haggle over prices with supercilious nobles and their imperious wives, against surrendering right and justice to the man of money. Poverty is the natural state of the rebel businessman rejecting his past and his self.

Francis espoused his beautiful Lady in a ceremony which is, I fear, only an allegorical short story, but was told as fact. Lady Poverty received her suitor and his train on a high mountain, and instructed them in edifying words. All descended to their mean settlement, and to cleanse the Lady's hands gave her water in their one un-cracked bowl. As they had no towel to dry her hands, a brother offered his tunic. They dined, on a few morsels of rye bread disposed on some handfuls of greens, pieced out with herbs gathered in the forest. Then she slept on the ground, with a stone for pillow.

How proud they were in their humility! And how gay!

Joy was obligatory in their little conventicle. "Why this sad face?" said Francis to a hangdog brother. "Have you committed some sin? That concerns you and God alone. Before me and my brethren keep always a look of holy joy, for it is not decent, when in the presence of God, to show a gloomy, frowning air." Sadness is a sickness of the soul, he insisted. The devils are helpless against a servant of God, happy in his devotion, but they triumph with his melancholy. So show a cheerful face to other men, and save your distress for God.

Recalling his early delight in hearing French ballad-singers, he told the brothers that they were God's minstrels, *Joculatores Dei.* Again he termed them his Knights of the Round Table. He bade them express in music their spiritual joy, which comes of cleanness of heart and is acquired by devout prayer. A fine singer himself, he led them in song, scraping one stick against another in substitute for a fiddle. In thought as in speech he was always something of a troubadour. Music to him was close to rapture. Once an angel appeared to him, bearing a lute. At the first heavenly strains Francis swooned with love and saw a blue Paradise opened, lit by the face of God.

His gaiety mingled with a pleasant humorous fancy. Once Francis and Brother Leo made a preaching tour. Leo fell ill, and craved some light and tasty food. It was summer's end and the grapes were ripe. Francis stepped into a roadside vineyard and plucked some bunches for Leo. Then up sprang the owner with a great stick, with which he belabored Saint Francis. The saint then made up a little rhyme, which he sang for days:

Frater Leo est bene refectus,
Sed Frater Franciscus est bene percussus.
Frater Leo bene comedit,
Sed Frater Franciscus suo corpore bene solvit.

Brother Leo has very well eaten,
But Brother Francis was very well beaten.
Brother Leo is stuffed, it's true,
But Brother Francis is black and blue.

The episode reminds us that Brother Francis, with all his contempt for property, respected the property of others as little as he did his own.

And we may remind ourselves that Francis's Lady Poverty was a country girl, accustomed to hard labor and hard fare, to rustic sights and smells, and to the annual drama of nature's renewal. Hers was not the poverty of city slums, with their filth, crime, and misery. Hers was rather the idyllic rural poverty of Christ and his apostles, who never seem to have lacked for food and shelter.

FIVE

The Poor Men of Christ

THE DOUBTS AND HESITATIONS that Francis revealed to his Master in prayer were largely dispelled by the enthusiasms of unsought disciples. Of such standing and character! The spectacle of noble LL.D.s donning the cheapest of gowns and doggedly thrusting all their wealth on the poor stilled the mockers. Many were moved to serious colloquies with Il Poverello. The clergy especially were eager to unriddle his spell, to learn the source of the strange compulsion he exerted and the clue to the mysterious joy of his followers, bubbling like schoolboys with a common secret. Francis could merely smile, and answer that he was following Christ's injunctions as best he might. His interlocutors wanted to argue the matter, according to the ancient Italian habit. Francis recognized that he must define his position, make public statements, or his brotherhood would risk trouble from some indiscretion of his own or of his associates. He knew his course was approved in heaven, but it was not yet approved on earth.

As the number of the disciples increased, they could no longer be regarded as a group of lawless eccentrics, withdrawn from society to nurture their souls in poverty. Disputes broke out among the brothers, huddled too close together. One could forgive a spiritual misdemeanor; it was hard to pardon a snorer, a bad-smeller. Some kind of organization, or system, was necessary, if time was not to be wasted in argument and harmony lost in disagreement. Especially it was necessary to define the relations of the order with the Church, which was regarding it with curiosity mingled with suspicion. Any religious movement outside the Church, uncontrolled by the hierarchy, was itself suspect, and the prominence or superiority of its members rendered it the more suspect. The Church wanted to know what purposes were in Francis's mind, and in fact we do too.

Francis had apparently gone beyond the mere proposal that the devout should give all their possessions to the poor and live lives of apostolic simplicity. Such a program, if generally adopted, would merely cause the rich and poor to change places, and would lead surely to universal destitution. It was suitable only for an elite, the physically and spiritually gifted. Francis held that the elite, following Christ's example, would in their turn set an example for the generality of men. All Christians would then be united in love and brotherhood, for men, aided by the infinite love of Christ, have only to perceive the good in order to pursue it.

But such a simplification of doctrine, a dubious one at that, was not sufficient for the wise old Church. Francis's scheme was too loose, too hazardous. He spoke without authority; he was untrained, unlettered, untonsured, not even an acolyte. There were no clerics in his first group of adherents, and no definition of responsibility, no chain of command. Worst of all, there seemed to be little place for the clergy in Francis's ideal world, beyond their necessary presence to administer the sacraments. He hated licenses, authorizations, official seals, in fact all stamps official or symbolic. He disregarded the accumulated wisdom of Church tradition and its treasury of virtue accessible to mankind. He seldom quoted or appealed to the saints, though he cherished a cult for John the Baptist, whose name, Giovanni, he had himself briefly borne in infancy. He invoked the Virgin Mary, though mostly in her role as mother of the Holy Child. His devotion was utterly given to Christ, for whom as his Savior he felt passionate love, expressing itself in an imitation approaching identification.

The doctrines of certain heretical sects of the time were not unlike his own. They included the return to the sole authority of the Gospel, the literal acceptance of Christ's commands, direct communication with the divine, the substitution of holy poverty for ecclesiastical display, propertyowning wealth, in short. In the case before it, the Church felt that Francis's beliefs, if unsupervised, might readily lapse into heresy. Perhaps they had already lapsed. The Church, recognizing his merits and usefulness, had nevertheless to assert and define its authority, hold him in check, guard against his characteristic wild outbursts.

And Francis's group, the Poor Men of Christ, had gained standing in Assisi. People grew tired of laughing at Messer Bernardone's crazy son; his words, when you came to think of them, were not crazy at all. Bad boys who threw mud at the Poor Men, jerked down their cowls from the rear, put dice in their hands and urged them to play, were reproved by parents and passersby. The brothers on their begging tours were asked to explain their purposes and principles. Francis, chiefly, was called upon to speak, in church porticos and on street corners.

The summons to make public testimony fitted his ambition, as yet unconfessed. When the members of his holy family numbered seven, says Saint Bonaventure, he called his sons together "and told them many things concerning the Kingdom of God, the contempt of the world, the sacrifice of their own souls and the chastisement of the body, and laid before them his intent of sending them forth into the four quarters of the world." What grandiosity of purpose, what presumption! Two missionaries for each of the world's quarters! And what a revenge upon the stupid world, which had denied him eminence in arms and in its esteem! Perhaps he recalled his own revelatory words: "I know that I shall become a great prince!" And: "One day I shall be venerated throughout the whole world!" Or perhaps he was merely indulging his propensity for dreams of glory. However, this dream came true, and now the myriad sons of Saint Francis go forth to the four quarters of the world, to work and pray for the glory of God, in honor of their founder.

He had his troubles developing a preaching style effective for miscellaneous or hostile gatherings. He was perhaps too self-conscious for the give and take of street preaching, too earnest to bandy jokes with hecklers. And in Assisi he was simply too well known; he confronted too many grinning faces of old companions. He must look farther afield. So, in lovely June of 1209 (or, as some have it, 1208), with newly converted Brother Egidio, he attempted a missionary trip to the March of Ancona, eastward over the great spine of the Apennines and down to the Adriatic. The mountains were yellow with broom; the larks sang overhead, and Francis and Egidio with them. But the peasants would not heed. By day they were too busy in the fields, and by night too tired to listen.

For Francis the journey was an important lesson. He examined his own methods of persuasion, his posture before the public. Recognizing his failures, he boldly created a revivalist technique of his own. But before launching a missionary effort he had to regularize his relations with the Church.

He obtained an audience with Bishop Guido of Assisi, who had covered his nakedness and quashed the suit brought by Pietro Bernardone, and whom he could regard as his friend. Guido is described as rich, proud, magnificent, energetic, imperious, violent, and litigious. He was accused even of using his fists in defense of the Church's rights. He was a fine type of battling bishop, and clearly he admired Francis's courage, while disapproving his methods. He did not absolutely forbid Francis to preach and make converts, but he pointed out the dangers in the young zealot's program, and urged him and his fellows to join one of the established monastic orders, wherein they could be as poor and self-denying as they pleased. But Francis had no idea of destroying his order by merging it in a greater, and no idea of subjecting his own will to that of an official of a Church organization. He could be as humble as one could wish in self-deprivation and self-discipline; but he could not and would not submit to any rule save his own, or that of Christ, or that of Christ's vicar on earth.

"We shall appeal to the pope!" he told his companions. When they shuddered at his dizzy temerity, he revealed to them a very convenient dream. He had seemed to be

walking along a road, past a gigantic tree in full leaf. And
he had seemed to rise up to the treetop, which he seized
and bent down to the ground. The brothers recognized
the good augury of the dream; they did not push the
symbol too far.

Filled with happy confidence, Francis and twelve of
his apostles set forth for Rome. It was the early summer
of 1210 (or 1209?), when one could sleep in barns or in
the open, when food was plentiful and readily offered to
worthy poor, begging for the love of God. Brother Egidio
kissed the grass, the trees, the stones, for very bliss. The
pilgrims followed the highway through the rich, jocund
valley of what was then the duchy of Spoleto, past the
ancient Temple of Clitumnus, embowered by poplars
and willows beside its placid pool, and on to Terni, and
thence by the old Via Flaminia to Rome. It was one of
those happy, singing pilgrimages that the brothers always
recalled with joy.

Francis carried in his cowl a proposed rule for his order.
It is now lost, and there is not much use speculating on
its contents. But the mere existence of a rule indicates
that Francis was ready to make concessions, that he was
prepared to be somewhat reasonable, to accept, like so
many rebels, the world as it is.

In Rome, Francis, never humble in pursuit of holy
ends, penetrated into the Lateran Palace, the seat of
papal government. He found Pope Innocent III pacing
to and fro in the Hall of the Mirror, meditating on, no
doubt, matters of high policy. Francis tried to obtrude his
own concerns and received nothing but the papal brush-
off. Fortunately he found his friend Bishop Guido of
Assisi in Rome on some ecclesiastical business. The bishop
presented Francis to the eminent Cardinal Giovanni di

San Paolo, for in Rome, as in other capitals, petitioners invoked influence upon influence. Cardinal di San Paolo was a man of piety and vigor, and was willing to wield his enormous power in furtherance of worthy enterprises. The cardinal received Francis and his companions in the Lateran Palace and questioned them closely. He was sympathetic to their purposes, but he concluded that the ideal of total poverty was too difficult of attainment, and that the zeal of the brothers would fade with time. Like any good organization man, he recommended that the petitioners should either join an established order or form a new one, properly regulated, within the Church. According to Saint Bonaventure, the cardinal reported the interview to the pope, saying: "If we reject this poor man's proposal to live according to Gospel precepts as a novelty, a bold challenge, we expose ourselves to impugning Christ's Gospel. For if we allege that to put in practice Gospel perfection is a novelty, a folly, an impossible challenge, that would be blasphemy against Christ."

Now the pope had been dreaming vivid dreams, as for instance of a palm leaf growing magically into a great tree. The symbolism was clear. And he had only just had another such evident warning in his sleep. He had seen his great Lateran basilica shaking crazily, as in an earthquake. And a weedy, insignificant monk had run and propped it up with his arm and had kept it from falling. "There," he had said to himself, "is one who, by his act and teaching, will support the Church of Christ."*

---

* Dreams are no longer divinely inspired — quite the contrary. Nor do the early biographers of Saint Francis pass the historian's rigorous tests of veridicality. One may feel that there are too many dreams and miraculous fulfillments in the stories. On the other hand, one is reluctant to dismiss out of hand the allegations of holy reporters. And in this particular case, Giotto has implanted in many minds the impression of

With Cardinal di San Paolo's report in hand (and, if you wish, with his own dream in mind), Pope Innocent received the delegates cordially, blessed them, and urged them to continue their good works and to preach repentance. He sanctioned Francis's draft of a rule. And he required the brothers immediately to submit to the small tonsure, an act which brought them under Church control. It was very likely at this time that Francis was made a deacon — his only ecclesiastical rank.

Surprise and doubt have been expressed that the mighty pope should have listened so readily to the ragged petitioners. Truly, the average pope would not have welcomed the average suppliant. But Innocent III was not an average pope, nor was Francis an average petitioner. This was a meeting of two great men, instinctively and mutually aware. Innocent, wise man that he was, recognized that Francis's proposal, however novel, was soundly based on common sense. And Innocent, having once approved the principles of the mendicant order, wished to get it under way as soon as possible.

The confrontation with Pope Innocent was one of the decisive episodes of Franciscan history. Innocent had devoted his life to fighting lay usurpation of Church privileges, and he was a consecrated champion of the Church's war against heresy. Francis's movement, with its implied criticism of the Church and its demand for a return to evangelical virtues, certainly gave off a strong odor of heresy. It would have taken only a little to tip the scales toward a condemnation of the Poor Men of Assisi — a new but upsetting dream, perhaps. If the scales had

---

his great fresco, showing the pope sound asleep with his tiara on, while the saint nonchalantly supports the tottering Church with one hand.

tipped, Francis would have been no saint, but a picturesque heretic, perhaps even a heresiarch, like Amaury del
Bene or Peter Waldo. Or he might have entered a strict
contemplative-ascetic order, like the Carthusians, and in
his austerities would have disappeared from history; and
Assisi might be now a half-deserted medieval village, and
there would be few Francescos or Francises in the world,
and we should all be the poorer.

Jubilant with their reception by the supreme pontiff
and with the success of their mission, the petitioners undertook their return journey. The sun warmed them and
Nature seemed to rejoice. The first part of their route lay
through the Roman campagna, fertile once but reduced
to a barren desolation, a dry, burned, hungry land. The
sun lost all its kindliness and played its hellfire role. The
brothers longed for water and there was none, for food
and there was no food, for they had resolutely taken no
thought for the morrow. But suddenly a man appeared
from nowhere, offered them a loaf of bread, and disappeared, like an angel. The brothers ate, and thanked God
for his constant loving care.

When they reached the beautiful hill country near
Orte, fifty miles from Rome, they found a refuge in what
was apparently an abandoned hermitage. They were at
ease, the citizens of Orte were generous, and they were
much tempted to settle permanently in this kindly, sanctified retreat. After two weeks, however, their master
warned that they were in danger of acquiring a sense of
ownership. They took lengthy counsel, and decided that
their duty was to live and work among men, not to embrace the delights of rural meditation. So, up and away
on the Spoleto road! (A Franciscan has nothing to pack.)

Then home with their good news, to the crowded cabin at Rivo Torto.

Possessing the pope's approval, or at least his refusal to condemn, Francis could now devote himself to preaching. He proved once more, as have many others, that effective eloquence depends somewhat on inspiration and somewhat more on technique. He possessed the essential for revivalist preaching — a fine resonant voice, a quick wit which could be trained to ready repartee, an appearance which stirred curiosity, and that kind of passion which could be roused at will. But he encountered difficulties on his mission. The churches were open informally for the public pieties of laymen, but one might preach therein only with the consent of the incumbent priest; and many priests were offended by this ragged, unkempt interloper. If he was barred from a church, his recourse was to preach in one of the town's few open spaces, and this too had its awkwardnesses. Once, preaching in the Piazza Comunale of Perugia, Francis's voice was drowned out by a band of knights practicing horsemanship and passages at arms. He turned on them and reproached them for their deeds of violence and pillage. But little they cared, if indeed they heard his words above the din.

"The Lord give you peace," he would begin his discourse. Then, in a strangely penetrating voice, in the colloquial Umbrian dialect of his country, he would approach his theme, perhaps the evils of war, the insolence of the nobles, the usurpations of the prelacy. Or, most often, the love of God and the beautiful drama of His life and death. Then his voice would rise and strengthen, and he would seem to be possessed by some alien, but holy, spirit. He would laugh and weep, play the characters he was describing; he leaped for joy, and uttered the word

"Bethlehem" bleating like a lamb. There are many testimonies to his power. "His words were like a flaming sword plunged into one's flesh," said one hearer; another: "He made of his whole body a tongue." Another: "He preached rather as an angel than as a man; his words were like sharp arrows." And a fourth: "His speech was as a blazing fire, penetrating the secrets of the heart, and he filled the minds of all with amazement, since he set forth no adornments of men's invention, but savored of the breath of the divine revelation." Such was his ebullient fervor, or, if one prefers, his pious kinesthesia, that he would break into dance steps as he preached. Invited to speak before Pope Honorius III (in 1220), he carefully prepared a sermon, but forgot it in the uplift of the moment and let inspiration take its course, bounding and dancing "like a man burned with the fire of God's love." His patron Ugolino, cardinal bishop of Ostia, was in terror lest the spiritual lords should laugh and mock him; but no, the prelates wept, "wondering at the power of grace and the speaker's assurance."

Abjuring formal pulpit eloquence, he spoke in conversational style, seeming to address each of his auditors personally. Most public speakers never learn this; they think of the thousands or millions of listeners out there, and forget that public persuasion consists merely of one man talking to another man. On the other hand, most of us cherish memories of great, though obscure, clerics, who spoke from the pulpit to our secret, grateful selves.

"His garments were soiled and torn, his person thin, his face pale, but God gave his words unheard-of power," said one who heard him preach in Perugia. He asked no aid of trappings, of fine vestments, even of cleanliness. But is that actually true? Did he not ask a good deal of his ragged, patched vestments and his haggard face, to set off the eloquence to come? He did not despise showmanship in a good cause. One cold winter day, after preaching in the Assisi marketplace, he adjured the congregation not to go away until he should return. He entered the church and stripped off his tunic. (He had some kind of compulsion about stripping.) He ordered a friar to drag him, naked, with a rope around his neck, to the marketplace. A second friar was deputed to carry a pan of ashes and throw them in his face when he should arrive; but at the last moment the ash-bearing friar refused to play his part. When the people saw their beloved Francis naked and hauled by a halter, they were horrified. But he proclaimed: "You all think I'm a saint. But I confess to God and to you that during my illness I have eaten meat! And meat broth!"

Everyone wept with pity and compassion. Some are still weeping. Others may be inclined to regard Francis's act as prompted by a morbid exhibitionism. And they may be impressed by his awareness of his living sainthood.

He felt, indeed, a pathological need for public confession and abasement. In a sermon he boasted that during the Advent fast he ate vegetables fried in bacon fat. His action is taken by modern biographers as "a scruple about sincerity; an exhibition of childish candor." But may it not be that his fault was not his breaking the Advent fast, which is not a very rigorous fast anyway. His fault was vanity, or pride, deadliest of the seven deadly sins. As soon as one conquers a manifestation of sinful pride, the trampled pride reappears as the pride of conquering sinful pride. Francis was well aware of this danger. Once he gave a poor old woman his cloak. Then he felt a puff of vanity, self-applause, pride, rise within him, and he proclaimed his repentance.

He knew well the menaces to his search for perfection. Chief of the menaces was the temptation to falsify his truth. It was said of him that his principal care was to avoid playing the hypocrite before God. That is a very difficult task, even for a saint.

SIX

Chiara di Favarone

WE PERCEIVE IN THE BLURRED CHRONOLOGY that the years
1209 and 1210 were eventful. Otto IV, newly crowned as
emperor by Pope Innocent III, made a triumphal entry
into Assisi, then went off to conquer Sicily from fellow
Christians, earning a papal excommunication on the way.
Francis, immured in Rivo Torto, refused to come out and
look at an emperor, thus demonstrating his contempt for
worldly glory. The pope visited Perugia for political, not
spiritual, reasons; he was probably too busy, and Francis
too indifferent, to arrange a meeting. The hostility of the
Assisan factions, the *majores* and the *minores,* was somewhat appeased by a pact of reconciliation. Francis was
admitted to preach freely in the cathedral church of San
Rufino. And he entered into spiritual intimacies, of
epochal consequence, with an adolescent daughter of the
nobility, Chiara di Favarone, whom we know simply as
Saint Clare.

Her family had all the appurtenances of nobility —
wealth and standing, several country castles, and a town

house in the fashionable quarter of Assisi. Her father and most of her close kin were hearty males, overbearing, quick to take offense, ready with the riposte. But the mother, Ortolana, is not so easily typed. She was no pallid anonymity, content to breed bravos for public or private battles. Indeed, for some time, apparently, she bred no one at all, and was afflicted by a shaming barrenness. She visited the sanctuary of Saint Michael the Archangel on Monte Gargano beside the Adriatic, and made the rounds of the wonderworking shrines of Rome. Then, with exemplary courage, she went as a pilgrim to the Holy Land.

This sensational trip must have been made in 1192, for, as the omniscient Arnaldo Fortini points out, only in that year did Sultan Saladin admit Christian visitors to Jerusalem. Ortolana took with her a girl cousin, noble of course, named Pacifica di Guelfuccio.

So summarized, the excursion sounds like a pleasant Mediterranean cruise. In fact, it must have been a triumph of will and endurance. Ortolana's first task was to obtain her husband's consent. No doubt she promised a stalwart son as his reward. But he must have been apprehensive of the separation, fearful of the privations, dangers, and diseases, and concerned about the costs. It was no easy matter to raise funds for the journey and transport them securely, whether in the form of gold or bills of exchange drawn on Palestinian merchants. The two mettlesome young ladies took ship at such a port as Bari or Brindisi, and underwent the usual miseries of sleeping on open decks in every weather, digesting sailors' tough food, and suffering seasickness. They landed, probably, at Damietta in Egypt, and then traversed on camelback the dreadful barren desert of Sinai. After a pause for recovery in the famous monastery of Saint Catherine, under

Moses's mountain, they continued through the burning desert to Palestine, to Jerusalem. Would that they had written an account of their travels!

They returned to Assisi, unscathed and joyful. Ortolana's prayers were answered with a small qualification, with regard to the sex of the child besought. In 1194, or possibly 1193, she was brought to bed of a beautiful girl-child, who was named Chiara, Italian for *clara*, bright, shining, gleaming, glorious. Few names have proved to be more fittingly chosen.

In her youth Chiara was familiar with violence and anger. The Favarone town house stood on the Piazza San Rufino, opposite the cathedral. The piazza was the stage for drama and controversy. The stone-flagged square resounded to the tramp of foot soldiers, to the clatter of cavalry. Below her family's loggia heralds trumpeted defiance; protesting commoners shouted, and sometimes fought, against their betters. Chiara may have enjoyed the spectacle, but she was terrified and revolted by blood and swordplay.

She had a first cousin, Rufino Offreduccio, who took his religious lessons seriously and was out of humor with the brawling bullyboys of his family. Once Rufino happened to be stopping at one of his father's castles at nearby Limigiano. He looked idly down at the courtyard, where stood two of Francis's followers, engaged in a very heated dispute. One of them turned out to be a new recruit to the order, named Barbaro. This Barbaro let fly at the other an unforgivable name, a fighting word. Rufino looked confidently, no doubt amusedly, for a combat with fists and feet, for the friars went weaponless. But to his amazement Barbaro seemed to take hold of himself; he knelt down and solemnly licked a little heap of mule droppings. He said: "Let my mouth, which let forth the offense against my comrade, suffer the penalty and the shame." Italians have always had an uncommon gift for dramatization.

Rufino was deeply impressed. He sought out Il Poverello, whom probably he already knew. A year later he joined the order in Rivo Torto.

Francis's method of character training was to humiliate the candidate. (This is, to be sure, the method of most initiations, even collegiate.) He thought that Rufino showed more timidity than zeal, and ordered him to go up to Assisi and preach a sermon in a church. (The church is unspecified, but it could have been the cathedral, San Rufino, from which the novice had his name.) Rufino begged to be excused, on the ground that he had no gift of speech, that he was ashamed to display his deficiencies. Francis then put on an air of ascendance which seldom appears in the *Little Flowers*. He peremptorily commanded Rufino to strip to his shorts, and go up and preach, preach! And preach he did, nearly naked, while the congregation roared with laughter — nakedness was not then so familiar as now it is — and muttered one to another: "Those fellows have done so much penance that they've gone crazy!"

Meanwhile Francis, reflecting on his harshness in subjecting to public mockery one of his city's important nobles, began to reproach himself. He murmured: "How can you, vile little man, son of Pietro Bernardone, have the presumption to order Brother Rufino, one of Assisi's noblest, to preach naked, like a maniac, to the people! In the name of God, you shall suffer what you impose on others!" So he whipped off his gown, handed it to Brother Leo to carry, and proceeded to the church, where the

near-naked Rufino was struggling to preach. Now, it is
well known that if one grotesque performer is funny, two
identical grotesque performers are ten times as funny.
The faithful of San Rufino had never had so much fun
in church. "But then Saint Francis, all naked as he was,
mounted into the pulpit and began to preach so mar-
velously on the contempt of the world, on holy penitence, on deliberate poverty, on our desire of the celestial
kingdom, on the nudity and the humiliations of our
Lord Jesus Christ, that all present, a great multitude of
men and women, began to weep very bitterly with incredible devotion and compunction of spirit."

If Francis's private reflections are accurately reported,
they suggest that he was still harboring his old resentment
against his father, who had imposed on him the ignominy
of being a cloth merchant's son, no noble. He was condemned by birth never to be first in Assisi. Very well
then; he would be first in the world.

The episode suggests further that his penchant for
stripping was not merely a symbol of the embrace of Lady
Poverty, not merely a psychological or pseudo-psychologi-
cal compulsion. It was a conscious effort to imitate his
Master, whose nakedness on the Cross is contemplated
and adored throughout the Christian world.

Brother Rufino's sensational topless sermon must have
been amply discussed in the household of the Favarones,
his cousins. Chiara listened eagerly. She was fascinated
by the stories of Francis Bernardone, who had renounced
property, standing, comfort, friendships, women's love,
to obey his conscience. She must have seen him, preaching
in church or walking on the streets of Assisi, and she must
have discussed him with her two younger sisters, Caterina
and Beatrice. And very likely her mother, who had left

home and family to visit the land of her Savior, took the side of Francis.

Clara was now seventeen, or maybe sixteen. She was unusually tall, as is evidenced by her handsomely embroidered robes, still displayed in her Assisan basilica. She is reported to have been beautiful, sweet, gracious, well mannered. She was enterprising; she even learned to read, and to speak some Latin. The Simone Martini and Giotto portraits show a lovely, aristocratic, intelligent face, and while these can hardly be invoked as proofs of beauty — for neither artist saw her in life — the portraits surely represent the recollections of her acquaintances.

It was high time that her marriage should be arranged. From her twelfth year, suitable matches were proposed to her, but she always found devices for putting them off. Clerical writers assert that she was consciously saving her virginity for Christ.

In Lent 1211, Chiara heard a sermon by Francis which profoundly moved her. Francis, no doubt, was putting in practice his gift of speaking to an audience so that each auditor felt the message was directed to him alone. She sought and gained an interview with the spellcaster. He sent her out in the streets to beg, wearing a veil and encased in a sack for a gown. She was the sort of girl who would enjoy such an adventure, such a change from housebound boredom. And did he not feel a little quiver of satisfaction at thus humbling the proud aristocrat?

With the connivance of Chiara's sister Caterina and her dear cousin Pacifica, she arranged meetings with Francis. He expatiated on a mystic espousal and chaste wedding with Jesus Christ, and vaunted the precious stone of virginity, urging her to keep it intact for the Heavenly Bridegroom. He counseled her to hate everything earthly.

She felt herself wounded, "liquefied, afire with the desire for eternal beauty and the possession of the immaculate Lamb, Jesus Christ, the longed-for Spouse," says her contemporary biographer. "She chose Francis to be her faithful paranymph, the one who should prepare her for the mystic wedding, and introduce her, brilliant and adorned, into the nuptial bed of the celestial Spouse."

For a year Chiara held sweet converse with Francis, always chaperoned, of course, but concealed from her parents' knowledge. She poured forth her naïve ardor; she begged Francis to let her take the Franciscan vows and adopt the Franciscan habit of a shoddy gown with a knotted rope for girdle.

Of course this would not do at all. It would be liberation with a vengeance, a disregard of the sex difference as unimportant. It would compromise Chiara and himself personally, as well as his order. Francis shared the monastic view that women were diabolically inspired since that business in Eden, that their chief delight was the damning of the souls of incautious churchmen. Tommaso da Celano quotes him as saying: "Except for women of tested virtue, it is as easy to talk to them without contamination as to walk through fire without burning one's feet." Tommaso continues that the Master's standoffishness with Chiara revealed fear and repulsion rather than prudence. To women generally he would speak only in monosyllables, with long silences, occasionally lifting his eyes to heaven as if seeking a check to earthly gossiping.

But despite Tommaso, one is forced to conclude that Francis's conferences with Chiara held their sweetness. He was twenty-eight years old, she seventeen or eighteen. She was beautiful, he was charged with spiritual force; the combination is explosive. She represented the distant, high-born, beloved lady of the troubadours who had taken his boyish fancy. Now she came, kneeling and humbling herself before him, and in her person humbling the noble caste which Francis loved and hated and longed to join, or, failing that, to humiliate.

Did Chiara love Francis, in the common understanding of "love"? Of course she loved Francis.

Did Francis love Chiara? No. He loved Jesus Christ; he loved himself. He was deeply attached to his friends, but he did not love them.

A year rolled on, and Lent of 1212 came in. On Palm Sunday Chiara attended High Mass in the cathedral. She wore her best gown and all her jewels. Bishop Guido officiated. At the end of the service he distributed the blest palms and the olive branches. But as the faithful crowded forward, Chiara remained at her place, kneeling, apparently oblivious of the external world. Bishop Guido, who of course knew her well, stepped down from the altar and placed in her hand the last remaining palm frond. This act seemed to signify heaven's favor for her purpose.

That night, still in her finery, she emerged from the family palazzo. A veiled figure met her — Pacifica di Guelfuccio, her cousin and confidante. The two descended the narrow, twisting streets to the city's walls, slipped out the Porta Moiano —

Wait a bit. There is something missing here. In Assisi, as in any medieval Italian city, the town gates were closed at sunset, and the keys entrusted to the mayor or his deputy. How were the gates opened to the two girls? Someone was bribed? But Chiara could hardly have raised enough money to bribe the *podestà,* and no duty officer, even if he held the keys, would have confronted the discovery that was certain to follow. There was some secret way over or under the walls? That would be hardly credible, with hostile Perugia only fifteen miles away. Yet Chiara and Pacifica did unquestionably emerge from the city, by human or divine aid.

The two descended the hill and took a designated road, or muletrack, through the woods. As they entered they were met by a band of friars carrying torches, who conducted them to the chapel of Portiuncula.

Then the rendezvous was fixed and the escape from the city prearranged, and the friars with their torches were privy to the very illegal enterprise. Since they would not have joined in any such plot without informing their master, Francis was clearly implicated. The rescue of a forlorn maiden in distress must have seemed to him very knightly. The only thing is, a Lancelot, a Roland, would not have acted anonymously, as if in fear of reprisals.

Francis and all who could crowd into the tiny chapel assembled there. In a torchlit ceremony, whether liturgically correct or improvised, Chiara and Pacifica were received into religion. They stripped off their ornaments, vain gauds, and laid them on the altar as offerings to the Virgin. They received from Francis their new costume — the shabby tunics of Minorite friars. At the climactic moment Francis produced a pair of scissors, or shears, gathered the postulants' hair, clipped it, and let it fall to the floor. The two had consummated their marriage to the Heavenly Bridegroom. However, Francis's assumption of the role of officiant was most uncanonical. Only the bishop was supposed to wield the fateful shears.

Then, by previous arrangement (by whom? and with whom?) Francis led the two new brides to the Benedictine convent of Saint Paul of the Abbesses, two miles away. The inexorable door closed behind them.

Francis walked back to the Portiuncula, exulting. He had rescued a soul from the wicked world, from perdition.

However, can one be so confident that the abduction was his doing? Did someone else possess the motive, means, and opportunity to arrange the escape from the city, to post the torchbearing friars as guides and guards, to arrange the midnight ceremony of veiling and the post-midnight reception by the convent? No one fits the role, no one but Francis. Readers may judge his act as they please — as the saving of a precious soul for Christ, as an act of intolerable presumption, as a touching example of chivalric heroism. At any rate, if his agency had been revealed, the scandal would have put an end to Francis's ministry and perhaps to his glory.

Back in Assisi, the Favarone family was at first too stunned to react. They took counsel together, and of course they recognized the instigator of the girls' flight. Within a few days, actually on Good Friday, they sent a delegation to the convent chapel. There Chiara awaited them. The delegates embarked on a prepared course of action, dwelling on their love and grief, then on Chiara's duty toward her family and ancestry, then, as tempers rose, passing to abuse and threats. Chiara took fright. In commemoration of the holy day the altar had been stripped, and was covered only with a white cloth symbolizing Christ's funeral shroud. Chiara seized a corner of the cloth and raised it as a defensive shield against her menacing kinsmen. The invaders shrank back, but shouted the more loudly. Then Chiara whipped off her kerchief, revealing her hair raggedly clipped to the skull. The abbess and her nuns hurried in and the importunate relatives fell back, abashed.

By this time the alarming Chiara had worn out her welcome with the peaceful nuns of Saint Paul of the Abbesses. The inexorable door turned out to be not so inexorable after all. She was shifted from one convent to another, ending in the Benedictine establishment of Sant' Angelo in Panzo, unless it was that of the Archangel Saint Michael. She soon found this refuge not to her liking. The nuns, good housewifely creatures, gave little thought to mystic ecstasies and the trials of the troubled soul, and spent most of their time discussing farms, rents, wool, cheese. She might as well have stayed home. At least Francis came daily to visit her, bringing her great spiritual solace.

On the Wednesday after Easter she had the great joy of receiving in her retreat her beloved sister Caterina, her confidante, her adorer, and throughout life her imitator. Caterina was now fourteen years old. She must have had all her mother's enterprise, in escaping alone from the prisoning palazzo.

This second defection was too much for the high-mettled Favaroni. On the next day a party of twelve males of the family, led by Chiara's Uncle Monaldo, a fierce old warrior, appeared at the convent. (Apparently Chiara's father was dead or incompetent.) As the emissaries gave indication of moderation and composure, they were permitted to see Chiara and Caterina, and present pleas for their return. Moderation was soon submerged in angry threats. Uncle Monaldo had sworn to bring back Caterina dead or alive, for she was not yet bound by irrevocable vows. He seized her and dragged her out to the waiting horses, then hustled her along the thorny, briary road, scratching her lamentably. A party of peasants, alerted by Caterina's screams, showed a disposition to interfere. Then Chiara, who had escaped, most illegally, from the convent, appeared, and by her eloquence and determination succeeded in obtaining the custody of her sister.

Now Francis decreed that the two sisters should be removed from their sheltering convent, where, perhaps, Chiara had irritated her hosts by excessive piety and aristocratic hauteur, and by the favors bestowed on her by Francis. But where could the sisters and their cousin Pacifica go? The answer came like a revelation — to Saint Damian's, the little chapel where Christ had descended from the Cross and ordered Francis to repair his house. Apparently the chapel was not arranged for the lodging and cloistering of nuns, but Francis was not one to be routed by formalities. Sister Caterina was inducted into religion under the name of Agnese, and the three girls were established in Saint Damian's as a kind of independent order related to the Friars Minor. The three, who were ignorant of conventual practice, and Francis, who cared nothing for man-made rules, acted with a good deal of freedom. He called frequently to give the young ladies holy counsel; and once, somewhat later, Chiara hinted that Brother Francis owed her an invitation in return. So, escorted by a group of friars, Chiara and another nun visited the Portiuncula. They picnicked gaily on the grass, nuns and brothers seated alternately, like ladies and gentlemen of society. It would be interesting to know what dinner was served.

The order was recognized as that of the Poor Ladies of Saint Damian's, later as the Second Order of Saint Francis. But as new recruits joined the sisterhood they took

Chiara's name as their designation — in Italy and France the *Clarisses,* in England the Poor Clares. In the early days they were subordinate to the will and whim of Francis, with small concern for the reproofs of bishops and even popes. Chiara liked to call herself "the little plant of Holy Father Francis." She would not admit that hers was a "second" order. In 1214 Francis named her abbess. By what right? He was no father, no priest, a deacon at most. But disregard of protocol was one of his charms.

Under Chiara's direction San Damiano prospered, but in a paradoxical way. Her rich friends insisted on making donations for her welfare and that of her companions; and she, totally imbued with the love of poverty, did her best to refuse them. She went so far as to petition Innocent III for the right to reject donations. The pope granted the request, remarking that it was the first time such a plea had ever come to the Court of Rome. Later, Pope Gregory IX, an old friend, tried to persuade her to accept a gift that would have assured her sisters' security and continuance. She refused angrily. The pope observed mildly that if she was troubled by her vows of poverty, he had the grace and power to absolve her. She had the audacity to reply: "Holy Father, absolve me from my sins, but not from my vow to follow our Lord Jesus Christ!" The pope received the rebuke with extraordinary docility.

But something seems to be missing in the recorded history of Saint Damian's. It was a tiny chapel, hardly more than a wayside oratory. During Chiara's abbacy it was enlarged to provide a dormitory and a refectory for a number of nuns, perhaps twenty or thirty, and also a crude charity hospital. The constructions are ample and clearly professional work; they have lasted unaltered for over seven hundred years. Someone must have paid the building and labor costs, so Chiara must have found some means of eluding her vow of rigorous poverty for her institution.

Her community was puzzling to the Church authorities. It was created haphazardly, by chance, not intention, and was governed just as irregularly. Francis himself had been taken by surprise. When he had welcomed the ardent runaway he had had no thought of establishing a new female order; he had merely obeyed mysterious chivalric impulses. Now the Church recognized that Chiara and her sisters in religion were doing noble work, and, the members being mostly of the rich ruling class of Assisi, that the order could not be suppressed without scandal. The foundation attracted young women of the *majores,* genuinely devout, but also unhappy in their imprisoning *palazzi,* and perhaps repelled by the rude, grizzled swordsmen proposed to them in marriage. The daughter of the king of Bohemia, even, applied for admission, but was dissuaded. Chiara's sister Agnese and cousin Pacifica were her first converts. Soon came the mother and Chiara's younger sister Beatrice. The gloomy house of the Favaroni was now stripped of its female occupants. The migrant ladies had made a new family home in the bleak cells of San Damiano.

If one is inclined to deplore the migration, the breakup of a family, and the thwarting of youth's normal destiny, one may reflect that youth's normal destiny is always precarious. A happy marriage for a woman is by no means assured today, and it was much less assured in medieval Italy. The consolations of religion are much surer, even though their fulfillment may be deferred to a future world. There are mundane consolations also. Chiara had the satisfaction of guiding her troop of sisters in the way of salvation, and of meriting the affection of a saint, the friendship and esteem of three popes, an intimate correspondence with the queen of Bohemia, and of course the certainty of God's favor. Saint Bonaventure pays her a typical tribute, saying that "that virgin dearest to God, the first plant among them, like a snowy spring blossom, breathed fragrance, and shone like a star exceeding bright." She had chosen the high way, the hard way, and there is no proof that she ever regretted her choice.

Chiara imposed her convictions, her rigor, on herself, and then upon her holy household. The first duty of the Poor Ladies was ritual prayer and praise; the second duty was work. Some nursed, for Saint Damian's became a sort of hospital, with the sick lodged, for a time, in a rude hut of adobe. There was always housework, with makeshift repairs to the home. Chiara made for herself a set of underclothes out of bristly pigskin to attain the acme of discomfort. She embroidered for Francis a white deacon's cassock, now displayed in the Sisters' Chapel of the Basilica of Saint Clare. Also on display is a pair of socks she knitted for Francis. Obviously he did not wear them much.

Life in Saint Damian's was grim, according to Chiara's rule. No time was allotted to reading and reflection. Those sisters who could read might recite the offices when someone should provide a breviary. The others should content themselves with repeating the Paternoster, up to fifty times, and they should make no effort to learn to read. There was no provision for recreation; those sisters who went into the city to beg or work were forbidden to bring back any news or gossip. Chiara's biographer boasted that in no cloister was penitence more rigorous and silence better preserved. Some of the inmates were so habituated to silence that they could speak only with difficulty.

The harsh routine of conventual life was occasionally lightened by the visits of Francis. He could let himself go among the nuns, indulging his taste for unexpected whimsicalities. He brought them once an accomplished pet lamb, and told this story: crossing the March of Ancona on a preaching tour, he had noticed the frightened creature in a herd of goats and rams. He took pity, and succeeded in buying it. (With what? Did he not violate his rule against touching money?) Leading his lamb, he called on the bishop of Osimo, to his surprise. He then trotted the lamb over the Apennines to the Portiuncula. He exhorted the lamb to piety, and it learned to enter the church at the sound of chanting, bending the knee and bleating before the Virgin's altar. At the Elevation it would bow low, setting an example for all the people. One suspects that the lamb's seriocomic reverence required long hours of patient training by its master. He then presented the exemplary lamb to the sisters at Saint Damian's. They made a robe from its wool and offered it to Francis, who kissed and caressed it with much feeling.

Such pleasing, playful intimacies were delightful to the nuns, who had renounced the intimacies of the world, and delightful also to Francis. He enjoyed startling his charges, though always in the interest of piety. Once the ladies besought him to preach them a sermon. After much demurring he consented. First, he prayed earnestly to Jesus Christ. Then he called for a pan of ashes. With these he drew a circle around himself on the floor, then poured the remainder on his head. He remained long in silence, kneeling. Then he rose, declaimed the psalm *Miserere mei, Deus,* and went out. "Thus he taught them to regard themselves as dust and ashes."

The sisters loved him tenderly, as he loved them. Yet he recognized the dangers of love abounding, or overabounding. Some brothers asked him why he did not yield more often to the touching appeals of the Poor Clares. He answered: "Don't think I don't love them dearly. . . . But if I am acting thus coldly, it is to set you an example. I don't want a brother to offer of his own accord to visit them; on the contrary I want supervisors appointed against their wills, men who show a certain repugnance, men of holy life, long known for their virtuous conduct." He guarded his little lambs with a solicitude bordering on suspicious jealousy. One cold December day Brother Filippo Lungo had the kindly inspiration to come to the aid of Francis, who had gone to perform some task at a convent, unnamed, but surely Saint Damian's. When Filippo appeared there, Francis fell into such a fury as he rarely exhibited. He made the unhappy friar strip, plunge into an icy stream, and walk, naked and dripping, the several miles to the Portiuncula.

By one of life's little ironies, after Francis's death Filippo Lungo was chosen as official Visitor to the convent.

Chiara must have influenced Francis in ways that are hard to recognize and define. She was a very good, courageous, noble woman, as well as a saint, and she set Francis an example in defying convention in order to follow the Lord's commands. Probably Francis had never known such a woman, exhibiting both inward and outward beauty. He had no sisters, as far as we know; he would not have been admitted to intimacy with nubile young ladies of the aristocracy. Probably the only young females he knew well were the wantons of the Company of Tripudiantes. Chiara, with her unaffected, unsensual adoration and fidelity, must have been a revelation to him. He may well have smiled at the small comforts she contrived for him, but they must have been welcome to his tortured flesh.

But evidence is scarce of Chiara's direct influence on Francis's life and mission in the world. It is true that when (in 1215) he was hesitating between embracing a life of preaching and one of prayer he asked her advice, and she urged the life of preaching. But he was seldom or never persuaded to action by others' counsel. The only advice he accepted was in confirmation of decisions already made.

The influence of Francis on Chiara was total. He offered her a revelation of her life's meaning and purpose. He taught her the joy of submission; he brought her sacred love, which must be superior to profane love. Certainly he brought her also grief and tears, to be submerged in spiritual consolations.

For fifteen years she lived in companionship of spirit with Francis. On the third of October, 1226, Francis died, at the Portiuncula. Chiara, immured by the imposed closure of her convent, was not present. Francis died in the arms of another worshiping lady. However, the funeral procession from the Portiuncula to the Assisi church turned aside to San Damiano. There Abbess Chiara was permitted to kiss the dead hands of her saint.

Chiara was already harassed by illness, which gradually worsened through the rest of her life. She bore with saintly fortitude her sufferings, being well aware that they were sent to try her. Obedient to the rule of closure, she never again passed the door of Saint Damian's. The incidents of her life were those, spiritual and material, of her family of nuns. One by one her companions departed for the land of their desire. Her valiant mother, Ortolana, died some time before 1238. Sister Agnese, Mother Superior of a daughter house in Florence, outlived Chiara by a bare fortnight. The younger sister, Beatrice, survived the two elders.

The outer world still made its intrusions, with visits from popes and clerical eminences and from those who came to adore the shrines of Saint Francis. In 1240 a troop of Emperor Frederick's Saracen cavalry descended on Saint Damian's, threatening irruption, plunder, and rape. Chiara was too sick to stand; she had herself carried out, bearing the Sacred Host, to confront the marauders, and they quailed before her. So the story is told; but the famed poverty of the convent and the starveling appearance of the nuns may have discouraged the invaders.

Her illness was aggravated; for the last two or three years of her life she was bedridden. Her friends contrived a padded support, so that she might sit up in bed and knit or spin with distaff and spindle. She produced a quantity of altar cloths and linen, especially for poor, remote country chapels. She carried on a long correspondence with the popes, protesting against a modified rule imposed by Innocent IV and insisting on her own rigorous rule. In 1253 Innocent visited Assisi. Moved by her prayers, he formally accepted Chiara's rule, and so informed her in a letter of 9 August 1253. Chiara received the letter on the tenth, and the following day she died. Present at her deathbed were Brothers Angelo, Leo, and Juniper, old companions of Francis.

Immediately after Chiara's death the pope set in motion the machinery for her canonization. Many testimonies to her sainthood were received, and the Devil's Advocate could find little to say. Chiara formally entered the ranks of the saints in 1255.

She was succeeded as abbess of Saint Damian's by a cousin, Sister Benedetta. With great energy the new abbess conducted a campaign to erect in Assisi a church to commemorate the saint and provide a home for the flourishing order. This was the Basilica of Santa Chiara, begun in 1257 and consecrated eight years later. The body of the saint was transported thither, with a pomp she would have scorned, and was hidden securely against relic-robbers. So securely, indeed, was it hidden that it was not rediscovered until 1850. She was found to be wearing a horsehair shirt; her undergarment was a mass of patches. A rib was sent to the pope, and pieces of bones to other convents of the Poor Clares. Her sorry skeleton, covered with simulated skin, was eventually placed in a glass tomb behind the altar.

Her splendid church is a fitting shrine for a saint in glory. Many, however, feel her presence less in the gold and glitter housing the horrid ancient corpse than in the chill simplicity of Saint Damian's, in the row of flowers marking her daily walk, in the bowl of broom set regularly at her place in the refectory.

Santa Chiara is now the patron saint of Italian television. This would have made her laugh. Perhaps it does make her laugh.

SEVEN

The Message to the Christian World

THE RESCUE — OR THE ABDUCTION — of Chiara and her sister and cousin, their entry into religion, and the attempt at armed liberation by their noble relatives were the sensation of Assisi in that Easter season of 1212. Francis had always been notorious; now he became Assisi's best-known citizen — pointed at, laughed at, or knelt to. From solitary outcast he had risen to be leader of a band of apostles, consciously reenacting the Savior's role. As Francis's standing among his fellows rose, his self-confidence and sense of mission increased. The mood was sharpened by the thoroughgoing reconstruction of the cathedral, dedicated to San Rufino. It stands proudly today. The work of building provoked an outburst of piety, and also of miracles, visions, prophetic dreams. Francis, no skeptic, doubtless took the supernatural swarming as indication that Heaven approved his cherished project, to evangelize the world.

He had always been convinced that he was born to some great destiny. With his conversion, with the divine injunction "Repair my house" in 1205 he had recognized his duty. The scope of his purpose steadily enlarged. In the winter of 1208–1209 he led his few disciples to the mountain retreat of Poggio Bustone, near Rieti. There he was ravished into a blissful ecstasy in which he was vouchsafed a vision of the future. He reported to his companions: "My well-beloved, be courageous and joyful in the Lord, and be not distressed by your small numbers nor by your simplicity nor by mine; for the Lord has truly shown me that he will make of us a multitude which will extend even to the ends of the earth. . . . [In my vision] I saw a great throng coming toward us to live our life under our habit, with the sole purpose of bowing to the rule of our blessed order. The sound of their footsteps rings in my ears; they were walking according to the rules of our holy obedience. I saw broad streets converging on this spot, coming from all countries. They were thronged with men hastening from France, Spain, Germany and England, speaking a thousand tongues!"

This vision has been and is forever fulfilled — although of course it may be spurious, the interpolation of a scribe transferring a fulfillment of later times to the past and crediting it to inspired prophecies.

With the affairs of his order prospering, Francis felt free to undertake the great work of conversion. His proposal was awesome in its presumption. He would Christianize the pagan world, with no equipment other than his own eloquence and the particular favor of God. If such a project seemed madness to earthbound Christians, he could reply that God had already sufficiently approved his madness, and that sacred history was full of examples of mass conversions, of the revelation of the truth in a moment to entire nations. As God had given him private assurance, he could not draw back out of fear and weakness.

Thus, in the autumn of 1211 or 1212, Francis and a companion embarked somewhere on the Adriatic coast, with destination Syria. That country was a mélange of Roman Catholics, Maronite Christians, Mohammedans and Jews. How he and his fellow traveler paid their fare is not revealed, but presumably Francis followed his old custom of taking no thought for the morrow, and somehow making the morrow obey him. The ship came to grief in a wild Adriatic storm, and found haven in Dalmatia. The captain refused to go farther, so Francis and his companion, being penniless, stowed away on a ship bound for Ancona. (He despised commercial morality and others' money, as he did his own.)

Some two years later he tried again, this time with the project of converting the Miramolin of Morocco, a ferocious enemy of Christianity. With Bernardo di Quintavalle he headed for Spain, but he fell sick on the way and had to return.

Francis was forced to recognize that the time had not come for the conversion of the world's heathendom. God had other purposes for him. All about him he saw religious indifference, hardness of heart, evidence of diabolical activity, sin. His duty was to preach to his familiar Christian society and leave the pagan world to wallow in its evil until the time should be ripe.

He was strengthening his position, particularly in making important, influential friends. Outstanding was Ugolino (or Hugolin, or Huguelin), cardinal of Ostia, the most powerful member of the Curia. He was a relative of Innocent III, and was himself destined for the tiara. He had the imposing appearance of a natural master of men, the courtliness of a Roman aristocrat, and the piety and blameless morals of a saint. He had also a firm grasp of practical realities, as he was later to prove, as pope, in his long conflict with Emperor Frederick II. But he chilled people; his spirit lacked ardor and warmth, and the abundance of these qualities in Francis cast a spell upon him. He became and remained the affectionate friend of Il Poverello and the protector and defender of his order. When visiting his charges he would doff his rich robes, put on their habit, and walk barefoot by their side. In rivalry with their humility he brought a leper into his palace and tended him with his own hands. Said Tommaso da Celano: "He was simple with the simple, humble with the humble, poor with the poor. He was a brother among brothers, the minimus of the Minores." Francis addressed him as "Bishop of the Whole Universe." During later troubled times, Ugolino may well have saved Francis's entire enterprise from dissolution. He supplied the prudent care that it was not in Francis's character to give.

Francis's second important friend was Giacoma (or Jacopa) dei Settesoli, a rich, devout, beautiful young widow of the highest Roman nobility. (It is noteworthy that the great protagonist of the poor made so many of his friends among the rich.) Her husband was one of the ancient, all-powerful Frangipani family, which by actual force had put one of its clan on the papal throne in the previous century. Giacoma's husband died young, and she was left to fight legal battles against the Holy See on behalf of her minor children. She was only twenty-two when she met Francis. He was in Rome on business with Pope Innocent III, in 1212 or thereabout. Perhaps she heard the Little Poor Man preach impromptu on some city piazza; more likely she was properly introduced in clerical society. There was no hint of impropriety, of course, but Lady Giacoma was said to have loved him. The *Mirror of Perfection* compares her to Mary Magdalen. She assumed motherly care of him, abolishing his revolting robe and feeding him dainties, especially sweet spice cakes called *mostaccioli,* later known as *crème frangipani.* Whether or not these contained mashed almonds is in dispute. In humorous defense of his friendship with the lady he called her Brother Giacoma, saying that she was a good Franciscan. Once, on quitting Rome, he presented her with a pet lamb, which was so well instructed spiritually that he followed his mistress to church and heard the service with great devotion. "If she was a little laggard in arising in the morning, he would come to rouse her, butting her with his little horns and wakening her with his bleating, pressing her by his actions to rise and be off to church." One remembers that Francis gave a pet lamb likewise to Chiara; and one wonders, perhaps indecently, whether Francis told Giacoma of Chiara and Chiara of Giacoma. This is none of the scholar's business, but even the sober historian may feel curiosity about the secret movements of his subject's heart. He may also guess; in this case the sober historian guesses that Francis told to one lady as little as possible about the other.

At some time during these years Francis found another important friend — Domingo de Calaroga, Saint Dominic. The saint had already founded his order of preaching brothers, known to the world as the Dominicans. The order, as yet small, bore and bears many resemblances to the Franciscan. It was founded to combat heresy and unfaith; its members were chiefly half laymen, lacking the priesthood; it was austere and ascetic, and attracted only those who were zealous to save souls, to serve God, and to affront martyrdom. But there were notable differences between the two leaders and between their orders. Dominic was a scholar, a theologian; Francis scorned scholarship. Dominic was an organization man, and struggled to have his little group incorporated into the Church's monastic system, in order to enlist its strength. On the other hand, Francis, suspicious of time-serving and self-seeking prelates, refused to accept the traditional disciplines, and would gladly have abolished all rules, making his friars subordinate only to Jesus Christ and to his own inspirations.

Cardinal Ugolino brought the two together and put to them a reasonable solution: "Why not unite your two little bands into a new order, stronger and more workable than either? As for its government, we could readily arrange to have bishops and prelates appointed from its ranks." Dominic replied that as long as he should live he would forbid his brothers to receive even the appearance of a dignity. And Francis: "My Lord, my brothers are called Minors in order that they may not even lay claim to greatness. Their vocation teaches them to keep on a modest level and to follow in Christ's steps, so that thus they may be elevated in the eyes of the saints." And as for a union of the two orders, Francis would not give it the least consideration.

Cardinal Ugolino considered himself edified as well as rebuked. The meeting ended in harmony; and Dominic asked and received of Francis, as a precious gift, his triple-knotted girdling rope. Dominic is reported then to have said privately to Francis that he wished the two orders could combine under a single rule, and Francis dodged the proposal. Naturally enough; if Dominic had really wanted a merger he could have offered to bring his brothers to the Franciscans, surrendering his own claim to leadership. If the two orders of friars had amalgamated, the intellectual and spiritual history of the western world would have required much revision. But neither of the two saints would renounce his creation.

The two remained good friends; Dominic visited the annual convention of the Friars Minor at the Portiuncula at least once. But he died in 1222 and the paths of the two orders diverged.

After Francis's excursions to Rome and far countries, he returned, in 1214, to the Portiuncula, and found affairs in prosperous case. After tending to business and admitting a throng of eager recruits, he longed to take again to the roads and to summon many sinners to repentance. He chose a new companion, Brother Masseo, and set off on the high road to the west. Coming to a junction, with signs pointing to Florence, Arezzo, and Siena, he seized Masseo and spun him about like a top until, dizzy and bewildered, he fell flat with his head toward Siena. So to Siena they went, and were enthusiastically welcomed by the populace.

Francis developed a technique of evangelical journeys. The brothers should walk two by two, not abreast but in file. So they continued to do for many years. Dante says that he traversed hell, walking directly behind Virgil, "as the Friars Minor go their journeys." Silence was imposed until tierce; but as that office was commonly celebrated in the smallest of the small hours, the requirement was seldom burdensome. Remember, commanded Francis, that our souls are to be treated as hermits in their mobile cells. However, the injunctions were often violated as the brothers burst into jolly songs and conversations by the wayside. The missionary methods are renewed today by Jehovah's Witnesses, whose adepts go in pairs to ring doorbells and report their revelations in intimate colloquies.

The entry of the friars into a town or village was a signal for rejoicing. Church bells rang as for mass. Children yelled; pious songs were sung. Men and women broke off branches to wave. The bolder snipped off souvenir bits from Francis's gown, leaving him sometimes half naked. The more timid esteemed themselves happy if they could touch the hem of his habit. Once at least he fainted in the press.

His first act on entering a town was to call on the bishop or other ecclesiastical authority. (In those days most Italian towns, however small, sustained a bishopric.) He would ask, and usually receive, permission to preach in the most capacious church, or, failing that, in a public square. Most activities ceased, and the citizens, devout or merely curious, assembled to hear him. There were few diversions in medieval towns, and men developed a critical competence in judging pulpit performance. The Franciscan procedure was carried on by American nineteenth-century revivalists, by golden-tongued preachers who stormed the country with a famous sermon to deliver. Such was the Reverend Russell Conwell, founder of Temple University, who gave his "Acres of Diamonds" over a thousand times.

It is a great pity that no one kept an informal record of Francis's sermons, and of the incidents, gaieties, and temptations by the way. The curiosity is often piqued. What can one make of the inscription reported to remain in the old Norman castle in Bari: "Here Francis vanquished a wanton young woman, or rather a raging serpent. In sackcloth and ashes he, by means of fire, extinguished the flames of a Venus risen out of the sea and attacking by the sea. In this castle he, the sturdy one, made the Cloister of Chastity impregnable."

What in the world happened?

We have also hints of strains and irritations within the order. Francis could be overharsh when offended, as when he punished a brother for touching a coin by making him take it in his lips and deposit it on a heap of ass's dung. Francis had a medieval penchant for scatology — or not so medieval; it is far outdone by modern scatology, which has at least the merit of permitting us to quote exactly, after all these years. An example: to Brother Rufino appeared the devil in the form of Christ crucified, to inform him that he was irremediably damned. Brother Rufino came in agony to his master. But Francis penetrated the demonic disguise, and counseled Rufino that if the devil should again attempt such trickery, the brother should reply merely: "Open your mouth and I'll shit in it." So it was done; and the shocked demon fled away in great wrath, in a mighty rain and tempest, with the rocks of Mount Subasio rolling and clashing down the mountainside to the valley, where they may be seen to this very day.

Brother Masseo, an uncommonly handsome, engaging youth, but rather a sobersides, was often taken aback by his master's unexpectedness. He once exploded to Francis: "Why you? Why you? Why you?"

"What do you mean, 'why you?'?" said Francis.

Masseo replied: "I say, why does everyone run after you and seem to long to see you, and hear you, and obey you? You aren't handsome to look at, and you don't know very much, and you aren't noble; so how does it happen that everyone runs after you?" Francis happily raised his eyes to heaven and seemed to converse with God. Then he knelt and praised God, and said:

> You want to know "why me?" Why does everyone run after me? The answer has come to me from the eyes of God himself, which contemplate everywhere the good and the wicked; for those most holy eyes have perceived among all the sinners of earth no one more vile, more insignificant, more sinful than I. And as, to achieve His marvelous purpose, He could find no baser creature on earth, for that very reason he chose me to confound the nobility and grandeur and force and beauty and wisdom of the world, so that every man might realize that all virtue and merit derive from Him, not from the creature, and that no one may glorify himself in His presence, and whoever glorieth glories in the Lord.

Then Brother Masseo was undone, and recognized that Francis reposed his spirit on true humility.

So we are told. We are not informed if troubling questions presented themselves to Brother Masseo's spirit. He could hardly have believed that Francis really thought himself the most vile and sinful creature on earth. He may well have wondered if the devil was not up to his old tricks, doing sleight of hand with virtues and vices, presenting sublime self-applause in the dress of humility.

The devil, with good reason, took Francis as his particular enemy, even his rival. (The devil has become today a comic figure, but perhaps that is merely his latest and most diabolical manifestation.) One day Brother Pacifico, praying with the Master in a deserted church, was rapt in a vision to heaven. There he saw a row of thrones, the highest one magnificent with gold and jewels, but unoccupied. "Whose throne is this?" he inquired; and a voice answered: "It was the throne of Lucifer, and there the humble Francis will sit." Emerging from his trance, Pacifico inquired of his companion: "What opinion do you have of yourself, brother?" Francis replied: "I think I am the greatest sinner in the world." By such a revelation of humility, adds Saint Bonaventure, Brother Pacifico recognized that his vision was truthful. At least it illustrates the esteem in which Lucifer, son of the morning, was held, and the surprising fact that in falling from heaven he had left his throne vacant since the world's beginning.

The internal troubles of the order are naturally minimized by the chroniclers, but they must be evident to the reader. In many regions the missioners met argumentative, stiff-necked heretics. Here and there the travelworn Minorites were themselves taken for heretics, and were tormented, robbed, and beaten, to return lamenting to their master. The clerical authorities regarded these street-corner evangelists with distrust, even contempt, as the established churches regarded the Salvation Army a century ago. And some of the Little Brothers were overzealous, too ready to criticize their hierarchical betters for their wealth, display, and rapacity; while some were underzealous, sick to death of walking barefoot over stony paths in the rain and eating the repellent scraps that fell from poor men's tables. At least, one could leave the order as one entered it, without formality, and many took advantage of their freedom. Among these was Brother Rufino, one of the first and most eminent recruits, who came to the conclusion that solitary prayer was more pleasing to a jealous God than preaching or service of the sick. He retired to a dank cleft in the Carceri, in the beetling mountains above Assisi, and there disappeared from the ken of men.

But the defections were far fewer than the replacements. Recruits came flocking in, attracted by the very excess of the order's demands. A properly devout young man in the mood for sacrifice wants to sacrifice all, not half; hence the popularity of the Trappists today. Similarly, the youth repelled by a career of money-getting is seduced by the prospect of total poverty, with the mere touch of a coin forbidden. He does not want to serve both God and Mammon, without even any substantial promise of reward by Mammon.

The order stood high in Rome, holding the personal regard of Pope Innocent III, the affection and approval of mighty Cardinal Ugolino, not to mention the support of battling Bishop Guido of Assisi. The standing of the Franciscans was put to the test at the Fourth Lateran Council, held in Rome in November 1215. Four hundred bishops and archbishops attended, eight hundred abbots and other prelates, and ambassadors from all the European powers. Presumably Francis was there, to defend the integrity of his order.

The pope opened the meetings with an eloquent plea for church reform and for the prosecution of the crusade (the Fifth) against the infidels. He quoted from Ezekiel IX (as recorded in the Douai Bible) :

"Go through the midst of the city, through the midst of Jerusalem, and mark *thau* [the last letter of the Hebrew alphabet] upon the foreheads of the men that sigh and mourn for all the abominations that are committed in the midst thereof." And to the others he said in my hearing: "Go ye after him through the city, and strike; let not your eye spare, nor be ye moved by pity. Utterly destroy old and young, maidens, children, and women: but upon whomsoever you shall see *thau*, kill him not."

Francis was much impressed. He adopted the sign thau as his own mark, or signature, since, like the Greek tau, it resembles a headless cross. He revered the sign, and painted it on his cell wall. Once Brother Pacifico saw it beautifully pictured on Francis's face in various radiant colors.

The council passed many resolutions, designed to invigorate the projected crusade, to correct abuses within the Church, and to strengthen the spirituality of the faithful. Alarmed at the proliferation of new orders, the council decreed that all such should accept either the rule of Saint Benedict or that of Saint Augustine. The last decree Pope Innocent immediately revised, excepting the Franciscans and the Dominicans. Dominic, however, accepted the Augustinian Rule, while Francis, characteristically, refused to yield to anyone.

Francis must have seized the occasion to lobby for his obsessing purpose, to extend his missionary effort within Christendom and beyond. The Little Brothers were already preaching in North and Central Italy, in Apulia and Sicily, and were sending scouts into southern France and Spain. Restless Brother Egidio (or Giles) had made the pilgrimage to Saint James of Compostela, and in this year 1215 he made the difficult journey to Jerusalem. But Egidio was more pilgrim than evangelist, while Francis had small interest in pious tourism.

Francis's plans received a setback in 1216. Innocent III and the Curia were in residence at Perugia, for political reasons. On 16 July Innocent suddenly died. As suddenly, the cardinals within reach deserted his body to elect his successor before the more distant members of the college could arrive. The eminent scholar-priest Jacques de Vitry arrived in Perugia that morning, and was shocked at the prevailing cynicism and license of the prelates. He called them "dumb dogs, not strong enough even to bark." The abandoned body of the great Innocent lay in state in the cathedral; and during the night thieves robbed it of its pontifical vestments and everything of value, leaving the pope half naked. "His body smelt very bad. I went there and saw with my own eyes how brief, vain, and ephemeral is the glory of this world," said Jacques de Vitry.

The interregnum lasted only two days. The Perugians, aware of previous year-long squabbles over the elections, and fearful of paying the expenses of a conclave with its hangers-on, announced that they would lock up the cardinals and decrease their rations day by day. Impelled by this spur, the electors chose a learned, pious, benevolent old Roman, who took the name of Honorius III. He was committed to carrying on the crusade against the Albigensian heretics and that against the Moslems in the Middle East.

Immediately after the election of the new pope, Francis, praying in the Portiuncula chapel, saw a dazzling light above the altar, and in that light Jesus and Mary surrounded by a choir of angels. And a celestial voice asked him what Deity might do for the relief of suffering mankind. Francis, as the basest of sinners, suggested that God should somewhat lift the burden of sin from His repentant creatures.

The next day, taking Brother Masseo for companion,

Francis walked to Perugia, and, with that compelling power of his, obtained an audience with the new pope, Honorius. As the admirable Arnaldo Fortini reconstructs the interview, Francis asked an indulgence for his new-built church of Saint Mary of the Angels, an extension of the Portiuncula chapel. (An indulgence is a remission or reduction of the punishments of purgatory, as assessed by the Divine Judge. The indulgence, for a specified term, may be gained by prayer and acts of contrition at a holy, accredited shrine.)

"For how many years?" asked the pope.

"I am not asking for years, but for souls. I want a total, or plenary, indulgence for all who may visit my church, repentant and properly absolved."

"But this is most irregular! It is unheard of!"

"It is not I who ask you this, but He who sent me, Jesus Christ."

"Well, all right. In the name of God, I grant you this indulgence."

Francis expressed his humble gratitude and took his leave. Honorius called him back. Did the brother not know that every administrative concession required a diploma, with signature and seal?

"Your Holiness's word is enough. This indulgence is God's work. God himself will make it public. Let the Virgin Mary be the charter, Christ the notary, the angels witnesses."

That very night Francis had a celestial message informing him that the indulgence had been ratified in heaven.

However, a great outcry arose among the cardinals, who thought the new inexperienced pope had been taken by surprise and had acted far too precipitately. A plenary indulgence, perpetually valid, would devalue all limited indulgences, even those promised to pilgrims to Rome, Jerusalem, and Compostela. It would injure clerical and commercial interests everywhere. It would practically put an end to sin! But the pope had spoken, and his word could not be revoked; it could only be amended and interpreted. Honorius was persuaded to eliminate the perpetual validity of the indulgence and limit it to a single day in a year. And even this decree, though ratified on high, was not properly registered on earth. Its authority was argued through several centuries. But still today the second of August is the day of the Great Pardon. Many thousands of pilgrims assemble from all Italy, and at the great modern Church of Saint Mary of the Angels, housing the Portiuncula, deliver themselves to hysterical ecstasies of penance, self-castigation, gratitude, and promise.

The growth of the Minorite order, the looseness of administration, and the difficulties of communication induced a vexatious loss of energy. Francis therefore decreed that his brothers should assemble at the Portiuncula once or twice a year, at Michaelmas (29 September) and at Pentecost, or Whitsunday (which the Umbrians call *Pasqua delle Rose,* Rose Easter) . But as the order spread ever outward from Assisi and increased steadily in membership, the management of the crowds and the conduct of orderly discussion became nearly impossible. The assemblies were therefore held biennially or triennially, with the effective decisions in the hands of small committees, as in our trade and professional conventions. The gatherings were now called *capitoli,* or chapters. Such recurrent conventions were a familiar monastic institution, already in vogue among the Cistercians and the Trinitarians.

The most celebrated of the chapters was the Chapter

of the Mats. Its date is uncertain, but it was typical of all the successful assemblies. The *Little Flowers* reports that five thousand Franciscans attended, but medieval estimates of numbers are sure to be too large and too round. This army encamped on the level fields and fallow around the original Saint Mary of the Angels. The local committee had done its best to provide quarters by erecting temporary reed huts and fitting them with straw mats — hence the Chapter of the Mats. As it was summer, many slept outdoors, with a stone or a piece of wood for a pillow and their gown for bedclothing. But the commisariat, faced with unexpected demands, was close to collapse. Francis preached to the multitude, assuring all that the Lord would provide.

> The chief Shepherd, Christ the blessed, being willed to show what care He hath for His sheep and His singular love for His poor ones, anon moved the hearts of the people of Perugia, of Spoleto, of Foligno, of Spello, and of Assisi and of the other cities round about, to bring wherewithal to eat and to drink to that holy congregation. And lo, there came quickly from the aforesaid cities men with sumpter mules and horses and carts, loaded with bread and wine, with beans and cheese and other good things to eat, according to the needs of Christ's poor ones. Besides this they brought napery and pitchers and bowls and glasses, and other vessels needful for so great a multitude; and blessed he that could bring the heaviest load or serve most diligently, so that knights and barons also and other noblemen who had come to look on served them with great humility and devotion.

The delegates divided into discussion groups of sixty, a hundred, or more. They prayed, said the offices, bewailed their sins or those of their benefactors, and discoursed of God and of their salvation. Dominic was there, much impressed; he took notes for the consideration of his own order. And the protector, Cardinal Ugolino, came over daily from Perugia. He would say mass, then cast off his sumptuous cloak, which was probably very warm anyway, and his shoes. "Truly this is the camp and army of the knights of God!" he exclaimed.

At the General Chapter of 1217 the order was divided into provinces, with a chain of command running down from "provincial minister" to "custodians" and "guardians," to avoid the connotations of the Church's official nomenclature.

Francis was now ready to realize his dearest purpose — to evangelize the world.

He called for volunteer missionaries, chose the most enthusiastic, and sent them forth on their perilous adventures. Their preparation was entirely spiritual, not at all practical. They carried no money, of course, and seldom possessed any knowledge of the languages of their destination. Not even did they bear any proper written authorization to preach, or any introduction to foreign prelates and governments.

To set an example, Francis chose to bring the Gospel message to France, the country of his special affection, to which he was in a way consecrated by his baptismal name. He gave as his reason for choosing France the particular reverence in that country for the Eucharist. With Brother Masseo for companion, he set out on his mighty enterprise in the summer of 1217. In Florence the two found Cardinal Ugolino, who gave Francis, as usual, the sound advice of common sense.

"Brother," he said, "I don't want you to go beyond

the Alps, for there are a number of prelates and others in the Roman Curia who would like to thwart the interests of your order. The other cardinals and I myself, who love your order, will aid and protect you better if you remain inside the frontiers of this province."

"It would be a great shame for me to remain in this province when I have sent my brothers into distant provinces," Francis replied.

The cardinal answered in a reproachful tone: "Why did you send your brothers so far to suffer so many trials and to die of hunger?"

Francis spoke prophetic words: "Your Eminence, do you then think and believe that the Lord God sent brothers for this province alone? I tell you that in fact God has chosen and sent the brothers for the profit and salvation of all mankind. They will be welcomed not only in the lands of the faith, but in those of infidels. Let them keep their promises to God, and God will answer all their needs."

Nevertheless, after reflection Francis recognized that Cardinal Ugolino was quite right. He returned to his base at Assisi and deputed Brother Pacifico to the French mission. Pacifico was the former troubadour; but in France the fact of his crowning as King of Verse by the German emperor was no recommendation. He of course knew Provençal, and may have betrayed sympathy for his French fellow poets, in large part Albigensians. He and his party immediately came under suspicion as heretics. They were forbidden to speak in public, and were kept in Paris under a kind of house arrest until, nearly two years later, they were cleared by a message from the pope. In 1223 or 1224 Pacifico was succeeded in the Paris governorship, or "ministry," by Gregory of Naples. He built a large, handsome headquarters building on the site of the present Luxembourg. When Francis learned of this infidelity to Lady Poverty he ordered the building torn down, but it fell down, anyway, before it could be occupied. (Medieval architecture had its failures as well as its triumphs, but the failures have returned to rubble.) In spite of this ominous beginning the Paris province prospered, and the restored convent became a great center of philosophical and theological thought throughout the thirteenth century.

France was for the early missionaries a warm, welcoming land, with an easily learned language, a widespread mood of intellectual curiosity, and assimilable food and drink. Germany was something else. One had first to pass the terrible Alps, and then fall into the grip of a race animated by the *furor teutonicus* and communicating in a harsh, throaty language. Giovanni di Penna and about sixty brothers, none of them German-speaking, invaded the North, evidently in 1217. When the Germans addressed them with a rising inflection, presumably saying: *"Wollt Ihr etwas essen?"* or something of the sort, they answered: *"Ja, ja!"* and were fed. But when people put to them crucial questions like: "Are you heretics? Have you come to pervert Germany as you have led Lombardy astray?" they continued to reply eagerly: *"Ja, ja!"* Then some were beaten, some were put in the pillory, and some were paraded naked before the populace. They turned tail and fled to Italy, to report that Germany was a cruel country, and that no one should go there unless harried by a longing for martyrdom.

Four years later a better-prepared expedition was launched. When, in chapter, volunteers were sought, ninety stood up. A timid brother, Giordano da Giano, fascinated by their self-sacrificing zeal, accosted them, saying: "Who are you? Where do you come from?" He confessed that he was looking forward to the time when the inevitable news of their martyrdom should arrive; it would then be a great glory to him if he could offhandedly remark: "Why, I knew him personally!" But, mingling with the volunteers, he was carried away by their enthusiasm and found himself standing among the chosen, and he was too shamed to withdraw. So off he went with the party, which assembled at Trent by the end of September, under the leadership of a competent scholar, Brother Caesar of Speyer, a German, with several German-speaking recruits. They started very gaily over the Brenner pass. But the mountain chill descended, and from the inhabitants of this still touchy borderland these exuberant Italians got only sour looks and no charity. They dined on two rolls and seven turnips, and at last, nibbling on berries and roots, came stumbling into Augsburg, where they were kindly received and well fed by the bishop. The missioners found their way to German hearts, and ever since Germany has been one of the strongholds of Franciscanism.

But there were awkwardnesses. Caesar of Speyer possessed the compelling power of the true converter; he persuaded many laymen to join the current crusade in Egypt against the Moslems. When the crusade failed and the surviving Christian volunteers returned, ruined in health and fortune, their wives attacked Caesar of Speyer and drove him to seek refuge among the Moslems of Syria.

The mission to England was postponed, no doubt because of the remoteness of the island. In September 1224 nine Franciscans landed at Dover, in a boat borrowed from the French Benedictines. Canterbury, London, and particularly Oxford became Franciscan centers. Those who attended courses at Oxford University had sometimes to wade through knee-deep swamps or trudge barefoot through the snow. The brothers in London lodged in dreadful Stinking Lane, Newgate. There they had sometimes no recourse against the cold but to huddle close together, like pigs. But in spite of all, the numbers, the morale, and the prestige of the "Greyfriars" remained high until the dissolution of the monasteries in 1535.

In Portugal the order gained the favor of Queen Urraca, with permission to settle in Lisbon and elsewhere. (There is a good story illustrating, among other things, an ill-mannered antifeminism rife among the elect. A noble lady asked a friar to be her spiritual director. He bade her bring a bundle of straw. This he ignited before her, and drew the lesson: "God's servant profits no more from consorting with women than does straw from consorting with fire.")

A delegation sent to Hungary came promptly to grief. The wild shepherds set their dogs on them, and prodded them with their crooks and staves. "Why do they mistreat us so?" asked a brother. "Perhaps they want our cloaks," suggested another. So they handed over their cloaks, and were beaten all the harder. "Perhaps it's our gowns they want," said a third. They made an offering of their gowns, and the blows were redoubled. "It must be our breeches they're after," said a friar. This last recourse was tried; the missionaries were allowed to escape. "One of the brothers told me that he had thus lost his breeches fifteen times," reported Giordano da Giano. "From modesty and shame he suffered more from this loss than from that of his other garments. Then he smeared his breeches with cow-dung and other filth, and the shepherds, disgusted, left them alone. Affected by this ill treatment and other affronts the brothers returned to Italy."

But persecution cannot daunt those who seek persecution for God's sake. The Franciscan seed was zealously cultivated in many Christian lands. The movement suffered many drawbacks of organization. It had no managing director, no central office, no staff to keep and file records, respond to urgent questions. The prohibition of money was a desperate inconvenience. Even paper, parchment, ink, had to be begged. One could hardly expect a newly appointed official to beg his way from Assisi to Oxford. The only person empowered to define principles and settle questions of policy was Francis himself, and he was seldom in the mood for administrative business. With his brothers far away, he was quit of their squabbles and distresses. Like Christ himself, he would do without administration. He could devote himself to his great project — to bring the faith to unbelievers dwelling in darkness, salvation to the heathen, Christ's message to the entire world.

EIGHT

The Message to the Moslems

FRANCIS was a *simpliste* — a word we need in English. He thought in large, simple generalizations, without distinctions and qualifications. Since, he assumed, the Christian revelation is indubitably true, and since men indubitably cleave to the true and reject the false, the Christian has only to present his truth to those who sit in darkness; the benighted will turn automatically to the light. Francis had proved his case among nominal Christians, corrupted though they were by heretical doctrinaires and cynical men of the world. So stout in the faith himself, he could not conceive that any reasonable man would refuse it. He could foresee a great surge of faith engulfing the whole earth.

Ideally, Francis should send his Little Brothers throughout the heathen world, preaching in the highways and byways, till the earth should be full of the knowledge of the Lord, as the waters cover the sea. But the method was hardly practical. His agents were all too few, the aid of grace not absolutely assured; and there was the language difficulty; and the rulers were hostile. There was an alternative, however — to convert the rulers, and through them their subjects, as did the great missionary saints of the early Church. Now at this time there was a whole world ready to receive the light — the Moslem world; and some at least of its rulers were reputed to be shaken in their fidelity to the Prophet, ripe to receive the true Word. There were rumors that Malik al-Zahir Ghazi, sultan of Aleppo and son of the great Saladin, was wavering. Pope Innocent III had carried on polite negotiations with Moslem potentates, looking to the exchange of prisoners. Commerce with the world of Islam and beyond flourished, entailing contacts with governmental officials. There was much speculation on the imminent downfall of the Mohammedan empire, with soothsayers basing their calculations on the Islamic calendar and on the Number of the Beast in Revelations. And Francis may have been stirred by the stories of Chiara's mother's sensational pilgrimage to Jerusalem and of her cordial reception there.

At this time (about 1218) the Saracens had recaptured most of Palestine, except for a strip along the coast — that same strip that is still a world trouble spot. Jerusalem was in the hands of the Saracens, but was usually accessible to affluent pilgrims from Christendom. Franks and Moslems had found a *modus vivendi,* and normally lived together in peace, to their mutual advantage. The throne of the Christian king of Jerusalem, which did not exist in physical fact, was occupied in principle by Jean de Brienne, brother of the Gautier de Brienne whom Francis had sought to join in Apulia, back in 1204 or 1205. Egypt was the property of al-Malik al-Kamil, a son of Saladin and a brother of the sultan of Aleppo. He had grown up in cosmopolitan Palestine and spoke French. He had been knighted with full ceremony, on a Palm Sunday, even, by Richard the Lion-Hearted, a good friend of his father.

This period of peace and relative good feeling was interrupted by Pope Innocent III, who proclaimed a crusade (the Fifth) at the Lateran Council of 1215. Recruiters, promotion men, money-raisers barnstormed Europe, and brought in many knightly volunteers, though the commoners held back. The crusade was aimed not directly at the recovery of Jerusalem, but rather at breaking the commercial dominance of rich Egypt by attacking Malik al-Kamil's capital of Cairo. The invaders disembarked at Damietta, beside one of the mouths of the Nile delta, in 1219, and undertook a siege. That city was strong, with triple walls, temporary towers for defensive archers, chains across the river to block ship movement, and stout-hearted defenders. The besiegers too were well equipped, but were hindered by unaccustomed heat, weighty armor, supply troubles, the rising of Nile waters, malarial mosquitoes blowing in from the marshes, quarrels among the allies, and dissensions between King Jean de Brienne and Cardinal Pelagius, the papal legate. The two were supposed to be on an equal footing — a bad arrangement in wartime — but the cardinal claimed supreme authority and an ex officio strategic competence belied by the facts.

The invaders suffered from another drawback — a lack of the old crusading spirit. Instead of freeing the Holy Sepulcher from the infidel, they found themselves attacking a well-defended fortress in a land that our Lord had never seen since babyhood. Their enterprise hardly seemed to merit divine assistance. Those who were animated by holy zeal were outnumbered by the greedy, the seekers for land and loot. Nor were these latter well repaid. Many regretted that they had not signed up for the rival Albigensian Crusade, which was richly rewarding the ambitious, in a land blessed with the best of food and wine and with perfect fighting weather.

Many of those who had served in Palestine were infected by tolerance for the Moslems, with whom they had dealt familiarly and even played and hunted. But Pope Innocent and stay-at-home enthusiasts were filled with bloodthirsty ardor. They regarded the killing of Moslems as an act meritorious in itself and pleasing to God, as indeed the Moslems regarded the killing of Christians. According to Church doctrine, Islam, born by the sword, must die by the sword. However, such a contention offended both Francis's hatred of cruelty and bloodshed and his gross, elementary logic. He asked if it would not be better to convert the Moslems than to kill them, better to save souls than to condemn them. They too were people of the Book, worshiping the one true God, respecting Jesus as a prophet second only to Mohammed. Half the work of converting them was already done.

Francis's ideal was fundamentally at odds with that of the crusaders. They wanted to cleanse the land of its pollution by eliminating the polluters; the less idealistic simply coveted land, money, promotion, jobs. Francis's ideal was to purify the world by correcting its errors, by the aid of God's grace, which would surely manifest itself in support of His agent's design. It was all so obvious! God was simply waiting for Francis to act.

Francis had, in fact, already broached the idea, in the chapter of 1217, of sending evangelizing missions to the heathen. Presented with all the charm of his eloquence, the proposal was fervently applauded. But sober second thoughts followed. The brothers had fortitude enough to confront cold and hunger, but by venturing into paynim lands they would offer themselves also to torture and death. Some of the brothers, not of the stuff of martyrs, whispered that Francis was really going too far. Time enough to think of saving heathen souls after so-called Christians had been brought to their duty.

Francis was conscious of dissension within his order and adverse influences without. Many of the recruits flocking in barely knew the Master, if at all. The new overseers (called ministers), appointed by the pope, were naturally prelates who had distinguished themselves within the Church structure, and naturally they would support Church tradition and scout the criticism implied in Francis's reforms. They were likely to regard Francis as an impractical visionary, a mere deacon, without training or scholarship. They thought his austerities beyond ordinary human capacities, and of course they were right. And his love of poverty was unwelcome, even incomprehensible — as incomprehensible as it would be in a modern course in economic theory.

Francis bore down all opposition, if indeed any was overtly stated. But he must have been aware that his followers no longer took his words as inspired by Deity. For the first time, or almost, his judgments could be argued, his commands contested. In the circumstances, he was probably glad to be quit of his administrative duties and to be off on the wildest of his spiritual adventures.

As usual, he had his way. He obtained from Pope Hororius official sanction for himself and a party to visit the battlefront in the Promised Land. Various other appointments were ratified. Brother Elias, the competent businessman, who was fated to succeed Francis in command of the order, was named minister of the eastern province, from Constantinople to Palestine and on to Egypt. To administer Franciscanism in this enormous area he had only one or two companions and of course no money at all. But Elias was not a man to waste his time in street beggary, or indeed in courting Lady Poverty. Surely he found a way of eluding the prescription.

Brother Benedetto d'Arezzo was sent to Greece, hearty Egidio to Tunis, with a companion, Brother Eletto. The Christian merchants resident in Tunis took fright at the missionaries' arrival, lest they should upset commercial relations by their zeal, as they certainly would have. The Christian merchants forcibly embarked Egidio on a ship bound for Italy. Eletto eluded the captors, preached, and was executed, holding a copy of the Franciscan Rule against his breast.

Six brothers were sent to Arab Spain. At first they were politely received, but in Seville they entered a mosque and preached against the Koran (in what language?). They were hauled out, beaten, and dragged before the emir. They defied him and reviled Mohammed, that wicked slave of the devil. They were then taken to the top of a tower (the Giralda?), whence they shouted down that Mohammed was an imposter. Jailed, they tried to convert the jailer and the other prisoners. Since the authorities could do nothing with them, the missioners were sent to Morocco, where, being still defiant, they were tortured and beheaded, as a divertissement for a ladies' lunch in the royal harem.

For himself, Francis had a fixed purpose — to confront the sultan of Egypt on his very throne, and to summon him to abandon his false faith for the true one. Would this conversion demand a miracle? Very well; he would offer himself as sacrifice, and surely the Lord would respond.

Francis left the Portiuncula after the chapter of Pentecost 1219, and joined a band of brothers setting off for their stations. At Ancona (probably) he found an army transport preparing to leave for the beachhead at Damietta. He applied for passage, and was granted the right to sail with twelve of his friars. He chose the lucky companions by a typically whimsical method — he asked a boy playing on the wharf to pick the twelve. The boy did his work well, whether by chance or by divine direction. He pointed to Pietro di Catanio, the noble jurist, two former knights, and Brother Illuminato, whose name in religion was well chosen. He is said to have been cured by Saint Francis of congenital blindness; and Dante caught a glimpse of him in Paradise.

The ship followed the usual course, by way of Cyprus to Acre in Palestine, the capital of all that remained of the Christian kingdom. Eleven of the Franciscans disembarked. After a pause for provisioning, the vessel continued on its way to Damietta, bearing, as objects of much curiosity, Brothers Francis and Illuminato. They reached their destination at the end of July, and found the camp in a bustle of activity, under the blaze of Egypt's midsummer sun. The Christian host, under the command of Cardinal Pelagius, was preparing a full-scale assault on the city.

"It won't work," said Francis. "The attack will fail. This the Lord has revealed to me."

One can imagine the scorn with which Cardinal Pelagius received this military judgment from an unkempt, insignificant friar, no doubt a saboteur, a wrecker of army morale.

The assault duly took place on 29 August, 1219, the day of the Decollation of John the Baptist. It duly failed, with great loss of Christian lives, and with the usual concomitants of horror. Five thousand Christians fell, many of them decapitated; for, says the chronicle: "Saint John the Baptist wished to have many companions, and so, as he was beheaded for God, an infinite number of Christians lost their heads." (This logic is rather startling.) The sultan then sent out criers with bags of skinned heads, advertising an important bargain sale of slaves. (If I understand this commercial practice, it is at least peculiar.)

A curious, though not very pertinent, item is that of the Christian women's corps. An Arab chronicler, Emad el Din, records:

> Among the Franks were cavalrywomen, wearing cuirasses and helmets and men's clothes. They threw themselves into the thick of the fray. . . . Being dressed in coats of mail, they were not recognized as women until they were disarmed and stripped. Some were sold as slaves; the old ones were always around and in the way.

These hardy ladies are not otherwise reported or identified. Probably in the lulls of battle they brought solace to the soldiery, and for this purpose had worked their passage to the front. There is a story that Francis was propositioned by a Moslem lady beautiful of body but sordid of soul. He said: "I accept; let us to bed." She led him into her rich bedroom, where a great fire was blazing on the hearth. "I shall take you to a much finer bed," said the saint. He stripped and lay close beside the fire, and invited her to join him. Untouched by heat and flame, he reposed with a radiant look on his face. The woman, thunderstruck, repented of her sins and her wicked purpose, and immediately accepted the Christian faith.

The Franciscan compendium of documents admits, in a footnote, that this anecdote is more picturesque than convincing. It seems that the item of the great fire in an Egyptian summer should give the critical reader pause.

The failure of the assault on Damietta did not dismay the stouthearted crusaders. The ring of Christian besiegers of the city was tightened; starvation did what force of arms could not do. Malik al-Kamil's large army, encamped upstream on the Nile, did its best to relieve the defenders, even disemboweling camels, stuffing them with foodstuffs, and letting them drift down the river to be picked up by the city's defenders. On 5 November 1219 the city fell to the Christians, and the survivors of its garrison were promptly executed. The booty, in gold, jewels, and fine textiles, was very rich.

At some time undetermined, before or after the fall of Damietta, Francis tested his conviction that persuasion could accomplish more than force. He had already found that by simply demanding an audience with the world's greatest, even the pope, he could so startle them that he would overpass all obstacles set by protocol and officialdom. Now, as he thought, the sultan, led astray by demonic counselors, was rejecting the peace offered by Christ. (In fact, the case was just the contrary; the sultan had proposed remarkably liberal peace terms, which Cardinal Pelagius had scornfully rejected.) Francis proposed to base his argument on fundamentals — the truth or falsity of the rival faiths. He had only to point out to the sultan his errors and the way of truth and salvation for his people and for himself.

The project was not quite so foolhardy as it at first appears. Malik was an enlightened Moslem intellectual, fond of science and theology, and particularly of mystical Sufi poetry, which breathes an ardent faith in God. He was naturally tolerant and humane; he had seen enough Christians in Palestine to recognize their virtues as well as their shortcomings. A Christian prisoner testified on his release that Malik had treated him as a father. The sultan later found a congenial crony in Emperor Frederick II, another freethinking intellectual.

Nevertheless, to beard the sultan in his tent was an audacious enterprise. The first necessity for Francis and Illuminato was to gain the permission of their military superior, Cardinal Pelagius. Francis had known too many cardinals to be awed by one, even in armor. The cardinal at first rejected Francis's proposal out of hand. It was too fantastic even to be considered. "If you go, you will never come back," he said. "If we go," they replied, "there will be no fault imputable to you; for you wouldn't be sending us; you would merely refrain from putting obstacles in our way." The cardinal finally relented, disclaiming all responsibility, washing his hands in the ancient metaphorical way, and no doubt feeling relief at getting the pair of fanatics out of his way.

So the two set out into the desert dawn, loudly singing: "Though I walk through the valley of the shadow of death, I will fear no evil, for thou art with me." It is no easy thing to change sides in wartime, as many a would-be transfuge has found. As one leaves one's own lines, some conscientious marksman is likely to pick one off; and as one approaches the enemy's lines one's cries of "Kamerad!" are apt to come too late. Brother Illuminato was extremely nervous; but Francis pointed to a pair of nibbling sheep and quoted: "Behold, I send you forth as sheep in the midst of wolves."

Soon enough, they approached the Egyptians' outposts. The idle guards roused at the sight of the strange, cowled, gray-robed visitors, who were shouting: "Sultan! Sultan!" The guards beat the two soundly out of precaution, but judged, on reflection, that they might be diplomatic envoys of some sort, or messengers, or deserters who should be interrogated. The guards bound the Christians' hands, and whipped them in to the sultan's camp.

Sultan Malik al-Kamil was bored in his palatial headquarters tent. He ordered that the mysterious visitors be brought into his presence. According to the contemporary chronicler Ernoul, they bowed low, and he courteously returned their bow. He addressed them in French; no doubt Francis had learned that the sultan liked to show off his French, as Francis liked to show off his own.

He asked them if they wanted to turn Saracen, or if they were bearers of a message. They answered that they would not become Saracen, but they had brought to him a message from God himself, that he should surrender his soul to God. "If you will believe us, we shall deliver your soul to God, for we tell you truly that if you die under your present law, you are lost, and God will never take your soul. That is why we have come to you. If you will hear us out, summon the wisest men of your suite, and we shall demonstrate to you by pure reason that your law is null and void. And if we do not persuade you that our truth is the only truth, we shall present our necks for the axe."

THE MESSAGE TO THE MOSLEMS ✝ 129

Whether by inspiration or by cunning, Francis had proposed the sort of theological discussion that Malik loved. He assembled his available imams and sages, and bade Francis speak. Says Saint Bonaventure: "He preached the Triune God and Jesus the Savior of the world with such vigorous thought and fervor of spirit that this verse of the Gospel was brilliantly realized in him: 'I will give you a mouth and wisdom, which all your adversaries will not be able to gainsay nor resist.' "

After this sermon, the sultan's counselors earnestly adjured him, by Allah and Mahoum, to have the blasphemers' heads immediately removed. But the sultan, who had enjoyed the saint's eloquence, and probably also his sarcasms regarding the Prophet, pressed Francis to remain and enliven his boredoms. Francis replied: "Sire, if you wish to be converted to Christ, and your people with you, for love of Him I shall happily remain with you. If you hesitate to abandon Mahomet's law for faith in Christ, have an immense brazier heated. I shall place myself in it with your priests, and you will then learn which of the two beliefs is the most sure and holy."

The sultan observed: "I doubt if any of my priests will be willing to expose himself to the fire for his faith, or endure such a torture." And in fact, says Saint Bonaventure, the sultan had just noticed an eminent elderly prelate slipping out of the room. Francis then offered to enter the fire alone, on condition that the sultan and his people should all become Christian if he should emerge unhurt. "If I am burned, blame only my sins; but if God's might protects me, recognize Him as the true God, Lord and Savior of all men." The sultan replied that he could accept no such bargain, since Francis would certainly pay for it with his life. But, having conceived a great liking for the two friars, he begged them to remain as his guests, for his intellectual diversion; and they could return to the Christians, loaded with gifts, whenever they should please.

The two stayed on for about two weeks. They were escorted back to the Christian lines under a flag of truce, to the amazement of all. Out of principle they had refused all gifts — with one possible exception. There is an ivory horn in the Assisi basilica, said to have been presented to Il Poverello by the sultan. Francis made a practice of blowing on it to announce that he was about to preach.

The visit to the sultan is corroborated from Arabic sources, but briefly and offhandedly. The friars are referred to merely as a pair of mad Frankish dervishes, who were received by the sultan with a courtesy beyond their deserts.

Francis and Illuminato remained in the crusaders' camp till early in the following year, 1220. It is not clear why they lingered; perhaps they were merely awaiting transportation to the Holy Land; perhaps they had taken the infections of tropical armies. Early historians of the crusades say that they were revolted by the soldiers' adulteries, robberies, and murders; "Francis saw the sin and evil which began to increase among the soldiers, and was displeased thereby. For this reason he left there, stayed for a while in Syria, and then returned to his own land." However, one suspects that the cause of his return lay deeper. He found himself at Damietta in an ambiguous position. Not even a priest, he could not administer the sacraments. Yet in his hours of exaltation he nourished the conviction that he was reserved for an overwhelming destiny, to fulfill God's dear purpose, to bring all Islam to the true faith. He would be one of Christianity's great converters, a Saint Silvester, a Saint Boniface. Why stop there? A Peter, a Paul! He must have mistaken God's purpose. Apparently God did not want to unite the world in His service, and He had not chosen Francis as his special, supreme agent. Apparently Francis was just the world's fool after all. And now God's fool too.

Francis is never quoted thereafter as recalling his Mideastern experiences. This silence may or may not be significant. It may be due to his unwillingness to remember a time filled with disillusion, failure, and shame before men and God.

So Francis and Illuminato said farewell to Egypt. The crusading forces in Damietta, contingents from half a dozen countries, spent a year and a half quarreling with each other, and finally, in July 1221, they moved cumbrously against Cairo. They were roundly defeated by Sultan Malik, who allowed the survivors to return, humiliated and destitute, to their homes, as a lesson to crusaders.

Some years later, the army's co-commander, King Jean de Brienne, of Jerusalem, renounced earthly fame and regal pomp for the shoddy gown and rope girdle of the Franciscan Minorites. His body lies today in the Basilica of Assisi, his tomb displaying the attributes both of pride and humility.

Rejoining Francis and Illuminato in Acre on their return from Egypt, we find them greeted by Brother Elias, minister provincial of Syria, and his little band of missioners. Among these was Caesar of Speyer, who had been driven out of Germany by the uprising of angry wives and widows of husbands whom he had persuaded to take the Cross. Elias and his group reported excellent success in their territory. Indeed, the eminent cleric Jacques de

Vitry, bishop of Acre, complained that the order was robbing him of his most earnest and competent aides. He continued that the story went that the pope's most trusted adviser was trying to leave the Curia to join the Little Poor Men. "I am convinced that if the Lord has resolved to use these simple poor men, it is to save a great number of souls before the world ends, and to shame our prelates" — of whom, one may remember, he had only the poorest opinion.

Now occurs a hiatus in our knowledge of Saint Francis's life. Where was he during the spring and early summer of 1220? How was he occupied? Did he visit the holy places of Jerusalem and its neighborhood? We do not know. Sultan Malik al-Kamil had given him a passport, or safe-conduct, for Jerusalem. It would seem inevitable that Francis, with his special cult for Christ and his life-long imitation of Him, would have made the short journey from the coast to the Holy City. Yet none of his faithful biographers mention such a visit, nor did the mention of Jerusalem evoke from him any recollections that have been preserved. Possibly he was lying sick and hidden in Acre. He was always inclined to illness, and he always mistreated his body, Brother Ass. He had contracted a persistent fever in the Nile delta, notoriously malarial. And the plague had declared itself during his stay with the army. And he was afflicted by the constant irritation of an eye trouble, which was to worsen until he went totally blind. This must surely have been trachoma, or Egyptian ophthalmia, which has been said to blind four out of every hundred Egyptian babies.

But if Francis was in a sickly lethargy, he was roused by news that came in July 1220. A brother, Stephen the Simple, had slipped away from Italy without authoriza-

tion and made his way to Syria to make a private report
to his Master. (He does not seem so simple as that.)
Francis had left two vicars in charge of his establishment
— Matteo da Narni, stationed at the Portiuncula to run
the home office, and Gregory of Naples, who was a kind
of traveling inspector. Of Matteo we know nothing; but
it was Gregory who, shortly after this time, built in Paris
a splendid but collapsible headquarters. He developed
into a harsh authoritarian, and was eventually deposed
and imprisoned. He was a nephew of Cardinal Ugolino,
the particular friend of the order, and thought himself
privileged to do what he pleased.

Brother Stephen's report was very upsetting to Francis.
Cardinal Ugolino was a kindly man, perhaps too kindly
to rule a group thirsty for austerity and suffering. He
was already supervisor of the Poor Ladies; under his direction they had prospered and expanded, with houses not
only at Saint Damian's but at Florence, Siena, Perugia,
and Lucca. The cardinal grieved to see the tender sisters
enduring unnecessary privations in following Francis's
example. He therefore imposed on the several houses the
mild Benedictine Rule, which Francis had always rejected
for his friars. A general slackening and loosening among
the brothers followed. Some of them were wasting their
time reading and studying; there was even a Franciscan
school of sacred studies in Bologna. Some were venturing
undue familiarity with women, eating out of the same
bowl with them. To be sure, trenchers for two were
normal medieval table equipment; but to what scandals
might this close contact not lead! A rumor of Francis's
death was circulated; and a strong party of rigorists profited by it to tighten discipline and cut off the liberties
of pious vagabonds.

Now Francis applauded asceticism, but voluntary asceticism, proceeding from a desire to suffer with Christ. He hated rules, and he hated being ordered about, especially being ordered about by previous subordinates in his own order.

At the frugal meal of the brothers in Acre Stephen the Simple read aloud the new constitutions. He came to a stipulation about fasting; meat was forbidden on certain days, and this was such a day. At this point a dish of meat was brought in. Said Francis to Brother Pietro di Catanio: "Brother Pietro, what shall we do?"

"Whatever you say, Brother Francis, for you have the authority."

"Then let us eat what is set before us, as the Bible bids us."

It was a sign of dissension, a tiny defiance, but a defiance nonetheless.

As soon as possible, Francis sailed for home in a Venetian galley, taking with him Brothers Caesar of Speyer, Pietro di Catanio, and Elias. They arrived at Venice after a fruitless and footless year, a year of dashed hopes, illness, disillusion.

But the Little Poor Man had his welcoming friends, in the fields and in the air. Says Saint Bonaventure:

> Walking with a certain Brother through the Venetian marshes, he chanced on a great host of birds that were sitting and singing among the bushes. Seeing them, he said to his companion: "Our sisters the birds are praising their Creator; let us too go among them and sing unto the Lord praises and the canonical hours." When they had gone into their midst, the birds stirred not from the spot, and when, by reason of their twittering, they could

not hear each other in reciting the hours, the holy man turned to the birds, saying: "My sisters the birds, cease from singing, while we render our due praises unto the Lord." Then the birds forthwith held their peace, and remained silent until, having said his hours at leisure and rendered his praises, the holy man of God again gave them leave to sing. And, as the man of God gave them leave, they at once took up their song again after their wonted fashion.

Where Francis walked, on the Isola del Deserto in the Venetian lagoon, now stands a Franciscan convent. Round about it the birds still cluster, jabbering excitedly, as if remembering and awaiting the man of God.

NINE

The Fool of God

IN EARLY AUGUST 1220, Francis left Venice for his home in the Portiuncula. As he was still shaken by eastern fevers, he rode a donkey. (Such possessions, which apparently violate his rule of total poverty, constantly turn up, without explanation, in the story.) In the dust behind him, encouraging the reluctant ass, marched Brother Leonardo di Gislerio, who had been in the world a rich and noble knight in Assisi. Tired and dirty, scuffing along, he ruminated: "It's a funny thing. My family would never have associated with his, and now he's the one riding, and I'm walking, and poking his donkey along." All of a sudden the Poverello halted and dismounted, saying: "You are quite right, brother. It isn't decent and proper that I should be mounted while you go afoot, for in the world you were nobler and richer than I." Leonardo, shamed, fell on his knees and avowed his secret thought, and pled for pardon. Later he testified to the truth of the incident at the posthumous trial of Francis for sanctification.

But how profound was the class feeling in little Assisi!

And how deep was Francis's inferiority complex and his resentment against the world's dispositions! And how scathing his irony, perhaps unsuspected by himself: "By humility I have outdone and outshone all you proud nobles!"

The two took their way over the hot lowlands to Bologna. Francis was troubled by rumors, assailed by concern about the events of his year's absence. Arriving in Bologna, he found that a convert, professor of law in the university, had taken over the Franciscan resthouse and had turned it into a House of Studies, in which he lectured on canon law. Canon law! What had a lover of Jesus to do with canon law? Had the Franciscans turned Pharisee? The defiance of all his principles infuriated Francis. He entered the House of Studies like a scourging angel, and drove out all the occupants, even the sick. To the canon lawyer he cried: "You want to destroy my order! It was my wish, and it still is, that my brothers should rather pray than read." On the quailing professor he pronounced a terrible curse, so terrible that the victim fell on his knees, begging Francis to take it back. The saint refused, on the ground that the curse had already been confirmed in heaven by Christ himself, and was therefore irrevocable. The professor, inconsolable, took to his bed. "And behold, there suddenly descended from on high a fiery sulphurous drop upon his body, perforating both him and the bed, and the poor man expired with a most frightful smell and the devil received his soul."

Whatever be the portion of truth in this anecdote, it presents Francis in no amiable light.

Pressed by a feeling of urgency, Francis immediately pushed on to interview Pope Honorius, without even a pause at Assisi. He found the pontiff with his court in

Orvieto. Contemptuous, as always, of protocol, he stationed himself outside the pope's door, and could not be dislodged until His Holiness emerged. Whether on this occasion or shortly after, in Rome, Francis asked, and obtained, that a protector, governor, and corrector for his order be appointed. He proposed the name of Ugolino, cardinal bishop of Ostia, his old friend and admirer.

Cardinal Ugolino did not immediately invoke his powers of reform, which were, indeed, ill defined. He contented himself with requiring a year's novitiate for entry to the order and with insistence that wandering friars should carry proper travel orders. Both requirements seem very sensible; they are, however, on the side of tightening regulation and control, uncongenial to the free spirit of Francis and his old companions.

Francis having retired from all governing office, Cardinal Ugolino, familiarly known as "the pope of the poor," carried on the order's routine business. He made some changes in the broadening structure of local and foreign missions, and he approved appointments and dismissals. Momentous was the elevation of Brother Elias to the post of minister general. Thus Elias's administrative abilities were recognized. But apparently unrecognized was his cast of character, which was practical, authoritarian, unspiritual — about as un-Franciscan as it could be.

At some time during this period — the dates are by no means clear — Francis had two painful shocks. Returning to his beloved Portiuncula after an absence, he saw with horror a new stone building rising among the huts and hovels, with a half-dozen Assisan knights watching the work. Raging at this defiance of poverty, he climbed to the roof, and, sobbing, began throwing down the tiles, while calling on the brothers to aid him. But the knights intervened, explaining that the building was the gift of the citizens of Assisi, to provide living quarters for the delegates to the chapter meetings. Francis, though sick at heart, could only desist, saying: "If it's your house, I don't want to touch it."

His brother Angelo, now an important citizen, was in charge of the work. Angelo constructed for Francis a private cell, of brushwood and rubble, perhaps out of brotherly concern, perhaps with a brotherly sneer. But on hearing someone call his hutch "*your* cell," Francis refused to occupy it.

The second shock occurred when a delegation of respected elder friars came to Cardinal Ugolino to complain of the disorder and disorganization within the movement. They asked Ugolino to persuade Francis to submit to the recommendations of the old, wise brethren, and to heed the admonitions of Saints Benedict, Augustine, and Bernard, whose works Francis had certainly never consulted. The cardinal, who probably had some sympathy with the complainants, informed Francis of the proposals at a general chapter meeting. Francis took him by the hand, led him before the meeting, and said: "Brothers, brothers! God has called me to walk in the way of humility and has shown me the way of simplicity. He has revealed this way for me and for those who wish to believe in me and imitate me. . . . The Lord has told me that he wants to make of me a new kind of fool in the world, and God doesn't want to direct us by any other kind of learning. God will use your knowledge and wisdom to confound you. He has his demon-agents to punish you; He has confidence in me. Whether you wish it or not, you will return, in shame, to your previous state!"

The cardinal, amazed, said not a word, but was conscious that all was not well within the order. The brothers trembled at their leader's vehemence. The dissidents did not, however, alter their views. When the fire of Francis's eloquence had died, many began to remark soberly that the order did in fact need some organization, if it was to do the work proposed to it. They may also have resented Francis's ability to read God's mind, which gave him an unfair advantage.

Apparently Francis spent the summer of 1221 in the Carceri, the cluster of cells plastered like a wasp's nest against a cleft in the side of Monte Subasio. There we inspect what is called "the smallest church in the world," nine feet by six, and beneath it Francis's oratory and his couch — an upthrusting bed-shaped lump of stone, four feet long. He lay there, thinking and dreaming, and dictating passages for a new rule for his order. His eye trouble grew worse. Once he recognized a passing shadow as Bernardo di Quintavalle, and called out: "Come and talk to the blind man!" There was no answer, as Bernardo was in one of his trances. To punish himself for interrupting, Francis made Bernardo walk on his throat and mouth.

The new rule took shape. There had been much complaint of the anarchic state of the order, without a constitution or even a statement of aims and principles. It is true that Francis had made a kind of rule about a dozen years earlier, but this has not survived; perhaps it was never written down. This vanished statement is sometimes called the First Rule, and the document that emerged from it in 1221 is the Second Rule. But as often, or more often, to the confusion of historians, the Second Rule is termed the First Rule, and the original pre-rule or Ur-rule remains in its obscurity, ungraced by any ordinal numeral.

The First Rule, then, the written rule of 1221, a development from the previous one, consists of twenty-three stipulations. Poverty, chastity, and obedience are required. For admittance to the order one must dispose of all one's possessions, and serve a year's novitiate. (The novitiate was a new requirement.) The Franciscan must wear a coarse gown and possess only books necessary for divine service. He will observe the fasts of Fridays, Advent, and Lent, but no particular foods are forbidden. No pride of rank is permitted; all Minorites are equal in humility. None may accept a post involving money or finance, but brothers may have necessary tools and utensils. They must not adopt a hypocritical, somber air, but be joyous in the Lord. None may receive cash. "We who have abandoned all, let us not lose for so little the kingdom of heaven." A friar who collects money is a thief, a Judas. Beg for food; alms are the heritage and right of the poor. Care tenderly for sick brothers. Do not judge, condemn, quarrel or criticize within the order. Avoid women; never converse alone with one. A fornicator is to be unfrocked and expelled. No pet animals are permitted.* On foreign missions, use tact — don't threaten. In preaching, accept the Church's doctrine; no innovations. Beware of the wisdom of this world, the prudence of the flesh. Come to the annual assembly, to discuss God's business. Practice regular confession and communion.

The rule then gives a sample exhortation, and admonitions to love, to lead the spiritual life, to practice the imitation of Christ, and miscellaneous counsels. The

---

* But Francis himself had two trained sheep, a crow, a hawk, and (possibly) a wolf. Rather surprisingly, he had no dog.

whole is interspersed with a mass of Gospel verses, said to have been contributed by Caesar of Speyer. The rule concludes with a celebrated lyrical prayer and thanksgiving — "Almighty, all-high, all-holy, all-sovereign God. . . ."

The rule is certainly a very fine guide to a godly life. It has been, and is, the basis of Franciscan conduct and practice. But one must recognize that Francis's morbid preoccupations show through — his horror of women, for instance, and his repulsion against money. Money, he said, was the devil in person. He did not attack the idea or principle of wealth, only wealth's innocent symbol and physical agent. We need no Freudian analysis to tell us that his hatred of money represented hatred of his father and rejection of his values, labors, and successes in the world.

The First Rule was presented by Brother Elias at the Pentecostal Assembly of 1221. Francis was ill. He sat at the feet of Elias and pulled at his skirt during the reading, to elucidate and make known his wishes. The dominance of his personality — mingled perhaps with love and pity — carried the measure through without overt opposition. However, no sooner was the First Rule promulgated than objectors, led by Brother Elias himself, began working to soften it. The rules of poverty were really excessive. A man had to have a knife, a spoon, a rag for cleanliness, for towel and handkerchief. Open sandals were very nice in summer, but in winter snows they encouraged frostbite and immobilized the wearers. The incidence of illness among the brothers was high; why was it forbidden them to have their own hospital? And the rule against touching money was really absurd; the Bible did not go so far. Time, in fact, seems to have justified the objectors.

The dissident brothers appealed to Brother Elias to try

to render the proposed rule more tolerant and tolerable. The pope did not give it his approval, for whatever reason. And Francis learned, of course, that there existed a strong countermovement within his own order, against his own creation. He was tired, lonely, and discouraged.

However, his illness lightened somewhat, and in that year he was able to resume his preaching tours, in which he found his joy. He found his joy also in suffering and abasement. It must have been in December 1221 that he recorded his definition of perfect joy, the most famous of his utterances (except "The Canticle of Brother Sun"). I give it here after the text of the *Little Flowers*. A recently discovered shorter version, regarded as authentic, makes of it a fanciful exercise, not a record of an actual occurrence. This may well be the truth of the matter, but I prefer the familiar text.

When then, one winter day Saint Francis was walking with Brother Leo from Perugia to Saint Mary of the Angels, the Portiuncula. The very sharp cold made him suffer greatly, and he called to Brother Leo, who was walking ahead, and said: "Even though the Minor Brothers may set everywhere a fine example of holiness and edification, nevertheless write this down, and note carefully, that that does not make perfect joy."

A little farther on Saint Francis called to him again: "O Brother Leo, even if the Minor Brother should make the blind see, straighten crooked limbs, drive out demons, make the deaf hear, the lame walk, the dumb speak, and — the greatest miracle — raise to life the four days dead, write that therein does not consist perfect joy."

Walking on a while, Saint Francis called out loudly: "O Brother Leo, if the Minor Brother knew all languages and all branches of knowledge and all the Scriptures, so that he could prophesy and reveal not only the future, but even the secrets of hearts and souls, write that therein does not lie perfect joy."

Going on a way, Saint Francis called out again loudly: "O Brother Leo, little sheep of God, even if the Friar Minor should speak the language of the angels and should know the courses of the stars and the virtues of herbs, and though all the treasures of the earth should be revealed to him, and though he should know the virtues of the birds and fishes, of animals and men, trees, stones, roots, and waters, write that therein does not lie perfect joy."

Then they went on a way, and Saint Francis called out in a big voice: "O Brother Leo, even though the Friar Minor should preach so well that he would convert all men to faith in Christ, write that that does not make perfect joy."

As these words had occupied them through a good two miles, Brother Leo, bewildered, asked: "Father, I beg you, for God's sake, to tell me wherein lies perfect joy." And Saint Francis answered: "When we arrive at Saint Mary of the Angels, soaked by the rain and frozen with cold, spattered with mud and tortured with hunger; if, when we knock at the convent door, the porter comes angrily and says: 'Who are you?' and we say: 'We are two of your brothers'; and he says: 'That's not true; you're a couple of tramps who go around fooling people and stealing the alms intended for the poor. So get out!' And when he won't open to us and he makes us stay outside till night, hungry in the snow and rain and cold — then if we bear all these rebuffs and cruel insults with patience, without answering back, and if we think with humility and charity that this doorkeeper really knows us, but God commands him to repulse us — then, O Brother Leo, write that there is perfect joy. And if we persist in knocking, and he comes running out in anger, to abuse and slap us and drive us away like a couple of obstinate tramps, and he says: 'Get out of here, you dirty little thieves! Go to the leper hospital, for you won't get any food or lodging here!' well, if we bear all that with patience and good cheer, in a proper spirit of charity — write, Brother Leo, that there is perfect joy. And if, pressed by hunger, cold, and darkness, we knock again and appeal and call him and beg and groan for the love of God to be let in, and if, more irritated than ever, he says: 'These are pig-headed rascals, I'll give them what they deserve!' and then he comes out with a knotty stick, and he seizes us by the cowl and throws us down and rolls us in the snow, and beats us with all the knots on his stick — if we bear all that patiently and with joy, thinking of the sufferings of the Blessed Christ, which we must bear for love of Him, write, O Brother Leo, that therein is perfect joy. And finally, hear the conclusion, Brother Leo. Above all the graces and gifts of the Holy Spirit which Christ accords to his friends is the gift of conquering one's self, and of willingly bearing for the love of Christ all burdens, insults, abuse and distresses.

Evidently for the true Franciscan perfect joy is a spiritual achievement, rewarding and justifying every sacrifice. Joy has ever been the mark and character of the order. Melancholy is "the Babylonian disease," said Francis. "Take your troubles to God, but when you join your companions, show only joy." Let your motto be *paupertas cum laetitia*.

Still today the visitor to Franciscan shrines and sanctuaries is moved by the gaiety and warmth of the brothers deputed to the care of their holy places. It must be that they have deserved and found perfect joy.

TEN

The Gathering Dark

By the spring of 1222 Francis was out on the roads again, expounding, arousing, exhorting. We have a precious description of his preaching style and power from the archdeacon of Spalato cathedral, who happened to be in Bologna on Assumption Day, and who remembered:

> I saw Saint Francis preach on the piazza in front of the small palace, where almost the whole city population was gathered. The exordium of his sermon was on angels, men, and demons. He discussed these rational creatures with so much aptness and eloquence that many scholars there present were no little amazed at the discourse of a man without culture. Indeed he did not take the style of a preacher, but rather that of a man haranguing the populace. The general tendency of his words was toward ending disputes and renewing the [civic] peace pacts. His garments were poor, his person mean, his face without beauty; but God inspired in him such power of speech that many nobles whose fierce discords had raged with great bloodshed were moved to make peace. And so in-

tense was the fervor that men and women flocked to him
in droves, and whoever could succeed even in touching
the hem of his robe esteemed himself blessed.

In Bologna Francis took the crucial step of reopening
the House of Studies, whose director he had scourged
forth with contumely. Regular courses were resumed.
Their content is not reported, but their mere existence
marks a surrender of Francis's antischolarly principles,
and a triumph of Cardinal Ugolino, Brother Elias, and
all the conventionalizing reform party. Similar schools,
or colleges, restricted to the priests within the order,
promptly appeared in Oxford, Paris, Cologne, and elsewhere, to the elevation of the friars in prestige, and to
the glory of Franciscanism through the centuries.

The Bologna school was put in the charge of the brilliant young Anthony of Padua, who has been called
"Christianity's most popular saint." (It would be more
exact to term him Roman Catholicism's most popular
saint.) His eloquence was compelling, prodigious, liter-
ally superhuman. For, according to the *Little Flowers,* he
was once rebuffed by infidel heretics in Rimini, and he
turned for a better reception to the fishes of the sea and
river. They assembled in a mighty multitude. "And all
held their heads out of the water in great peace and
gentleness and perfect order, and remained intent on the
lips of Saint Anthony: for in front of him and nearest to
the bank were the lesser fishes; and beyond them were
those of middling size; and then behind, where the water
was deepest, were the greater fishes." And such was the
saint's eloquence that "the fishes began to open their
mouths and bow their heads, and by these and other
tokens of reverence they gave praise to God."

If anyone doubts this, he has only to go and look at the pictured window in the lower church of the Assisi basilica.

Francis, who seems to have known Anthony only casually, had now a new project in mind. "There are too many Friars Minor!" he had exclaimed on returning from the Holy Land. Too many, too soft, too lacking in zeal, shamefaced beggars and hesitant evangelists. On the other hand, many of his most vigorous adherents came from without the order. Many laymen and laywomen applauded the principles of the Friars Minor and the Poor Ladies and asked if they could not share in the aspirations and consolations of the two orders. Would it not be possible to create a third order, which would encourage its members to lead Christian lives while remaining in the world? After meditating on this possibility for years, Francis broached the matter to Cardinal Ugolino, and the two drew up a rule for what was at first called an Order of Penitence. Though forerunners, such as the Humiliati of Lombardy and the Poor Catholics, can be discerned, this Third Order of Saint Francis was the first Catholic brotherhood, or confraternity, or sodality, or laymen's league, to thrive and endure.

The rule requires the brothers and sisters, soon to be known as Franciscan Tertiaries, to dress modestly, to avoid festivities and wanton games, to fast, and to do their religious duties. In all their worldly dealings they are to observe justice and the law, paying tithes and debts, giving alms, succoring the sick. They are to make their wills and to become reconciled with their enemies. And they are forbidden to bear arms, or to take any solemn oaths without the pope's consent.

The last requirements — which we may credit to Cardi-

nal Ugolino — have a special significance. It was important that a man should make his will, for the state, king,
or overlord would claim the property of those who died
intestate, thus balking the purposes of pious decedents.
Much of medieval behavior depended on oaths; an oath
invoked God as witness, and was treated as inviolate.
(The oaths of our law courts reproduce the medieval
forms, without the conviction that perjurers will be
divinely corrected.) A vassal assumed by oath his feudal
duties to his lord; if he could dodge the oath he might
dodge the duties. And if citizens could refuse to bear
arms, they would cripple the ambitions of cities and
lordlings, remove power from the Ghibellines, and trans-
fer it to the Guelfs — and the popes. In consequence,
hardly was the Third Order founded than almost the
whole population of Faenza joined it, to avoid service of
their sovereign in a hated war.

Even without such fringe benefits the appeal of the
Third Order was strong to tender religious spirits; with
the special advantages it was irresistible. Francis promised, on God's behalf, four privileges for the order: it
would last till Judgment Day; any persecutor of the order
would soon die; any evildoer who might enter the order
would be detected and cast out; any true member, however great a sinner, would obtain mercy at the end.
Though the fulfillment of the promises is at least argu-
able, the Third Order spread throughout the world and
had a phenomenal success. Its members included Giotto,
Leonardo da Vinci, Michelangelo, Velasquez, Rubens,
Cervantes, perhaps Dante. No other organization on earth
can boast such a list of alumni. But the present Franciscan
Third Orders are mostly clerical; other laymen's orga-
nizations have taken over Francis's purposes.

Back in the Portiuncula, Francis found his beloved home changed for the worse. His dialogue on perfect joy was prophetic; or perhaps it was the exaggeration of an event that had occurred in fact or imagination. A drowsy doorkeeper could perfectly well have failed to recognize him in the dark and could have demanded an identification. And within the shelters Francis could have found his welcome somewhat mitigated. Some of his old companions were far away on missions or in hermitages; some, as Pietro di Catanio, were dead. Others, now middle-aged, gave evidence of diminishing ardor. Francis observed uncorrected violations of his principles. A new spirit was rife, encouraged by Brother Elias, Cardinal Ugolino, and the pope himself. Less emphasis was placed on ascetic practice, manual labor, and personal sanctification, more on ceremonial, good works, and study. Francis discovered that his words were no longer taken as divinely inspired oracles. And he was now forty years old, already on the verge of medieval old age; and he was suffering the revenge of his mistreated body, Brother Ass. He came to prefer the solitary life of prayer and meditation to supervising the activities of the community.

Halfway between Assisi and Rome, round about the ancient city of Rieti, lies a most beautiful valley, the Agro Reatino, apparently the bed of a prehistoric lake. It is about a dozen miles long and as many broad. Ringed by steep mountains, it discourages visitors, and keeps itself to itself. Rieti sits among rich grain fields tilled by great white oxen; the mountainsides bloom with olives and vineyards, and provide footholds for villages set on narrow plateaus bordered by chasms and precipices. Above the villages, where the olives yield to oaks, are many natural caves, offering shelter to holy hermits. Masonry has extended the caves outward over the void, to make livable quarters. Some of these hermitages gained local fame, and villagers zigzagged up the mountain wall to feed the hermits, and erected shrines to them after their death.

Such a beguiling retreat, with chapel and livable additions, is Fonte Colombo, halfway up the mountain that protects Rieti. Its name means Doves' Spring, and the doves have justified the name. Here came Francis in the spring of 1223, bringing with him faithful Brother Leo, and also Brother Bonizzo, learned in canon law. The three had a specific task to do — to revise the Rule of 1221, which had never been formally accepted by the chapter or by the papal authorities. Objections were many, but most of them expressed the same prevailing dissatisfaction — Francis's rule was vague, indefinite, the statement of noble purposes without guidance for the searcher or set penalties for the transgressor. The obligation of total poverty was simply unworkable; it should be softened, to fit with common sense. Over half the rule's length was occupied with biblical quotations; now no one could hear Christ's words too often, but they were just out of place in the context. And so forth.

The three companions at Fonte Colombo made a draft of a new rule. No text of it persists. The fair copy was delivered to Brother Elias. And somehow or other he lost it. There is nothing surprising about that. Plenty of people were eager to borrow it, and every borrower was tempted to pass it on to another. And protective wrapping paper had not yet arrived; and a friar's cowl is no briefcase; it is made to be pulled over the head in case of rain, and then your manuscript is dampened, dispersed, lost. So Brother Elias could have lost the draft of the Second Rule. But the suspicion remains that Elias found it unsatisfactory and concealed or destroyed it. Assuming a new air of command, he told Francis that his version risked failure before the chapter and the higher authorities in Rome; and he advised Francis, out of his deep affection, to return to his retreat and prepare a more acceptable rule. So goes one version; according to another, Elias and other ministers protested that if the rule should prove too harsh, they would not be bound by it; and a heavenly voice attested: "All in thy rule is mine, and it is my will that it be observed to the letter, without commentary." If heavenly voice there was, the rebellious ministers did not heed it. They applied their steady pressure to Francis. And Francis surrendered, in one of those accesses of humility that in his spirit alternated with proud defiance. Or (I think better) he yielded in one of those accesses of physical and mental weariness that are common to all men. He felt old and sick; he was tired of arguing and fighting. Let others argue and fight if they would, and leave him alone.

This stage in his life is called by early biographers the Great Temptation. The term does not seem a very exact one; the period was rather the Great Discouragement, but perhaps it is called a Temptation to provide a parallel to Christ's temptation by the devil. At any rate a deep distress afflicted the Poor Little Man for about two dreadful years.

The distress was in part physical, or even the result of his physical state. He was chronically ill and in pain. His physicians laid the trouble to a deterioration of the liver, spleen, and stomach; their diagnosis suggests cancer. They were certainly right in attributing the ultimate cause to Francis's fasting, vigils, and contempt of all Nature's warnings and admonitions. His eye troubles, glaucoma or perhaps trachoma, gradually worsened, with a blurring of vision and a perpetual irritation of the conjunctivae. The beautiful world he loved gradually clouded and darkened, darkening at the same time his spirit.

To his physical distress was added distress of mind and soul. This was not merely the inevitable dryness, *siccitas,* of the mystics; it was the product of specific causes. He felt himself abandoned by his beloved brothers, who were at the same time abandoning his ideals of saintliness and seeking an easier, more comfortable way of life. He felt abandoned also by his dearest friends, by Cardinal Ugolino, by Brother Elias, who, in their ambition to make a great, powerful order, were ready to make concessions to human weakness, sacrificing divine strength.

It was bad enough for him to feel abandoned by his friends and companions. It was far worse to feel abandoned by God. Francis's prayers were unanswered, his soul unillumined. He was assailed by doubts and suspicions. He could no longer induce a state of mystic rapture; instead he found in his meditations pain, terror, glimpses of the devil leering in humorous triumph. Could he have been mistaken, all along? Was God's will manifested to cardinal and pope, while he was left a prey to ridiculous enthusiasms? Was he still, had he always been, just the simple, gullible son of Pietro Bernardone?

This testing of the spirit, this diabolical temptation to loss of faith, is familiar to all the devout, perhaps more familiar to great believers than to simple accepters of the faith. It is the dreadful, necessary Fourth Stage of the Mystic Way, the Dark Night of the Soul. Francis, a creature of his emotions, passed through racking alternations of feeling, from despair to disdainful pride. He beat his breast and insisted that he was the least and wickedest of men, deserving only of damnation. He was a worm, less than a worm. (True, he would allow no one else to claim superiority in insignificance.) He supposes that he may be ejected from the brotherhood as unworthy, and promises to receive such notice with humble joy; and the next moment he rises up on his bed to cry out against those who would steal his property: "Who are these people who have taken my order and my brothers out of my hands? If I go to the chapter I'll show them what I want!" But the Lord told him to calm down, not to worry, simply to tend to his own salvation.

He calmed down. His spirit was invaded by a slack listlessness, carelessness. "Let the brothers live as they please," he said. "All I can do is pray for them." Tranquil acceptance pleased him more than battle, even battle for the right. He learned, later than most people, the happiness of acceptance, of willing subjection. Perhaps he remembered how he had once given Brother Egidio perfect freedom, and Egidio had set off gaily to adventure. Four days later he returned, knelt to the Master, and said: "Father, send me wherever you wish, because my conscience cannot find peace in such a free obedience." And surely Francis recalled the revelation that had come to him with the knowledge of perfect joy: "Above all the gifts and graces of the Holy Spirit is the gift of conquering one's self." This gift was now granted him — but at what a price!

Suddenly the cloud was lifted. As Tommaso da Celano records the event, Francis had returned to the Portiuncula. Torturing himself, physically and spiritually, he wept bitterly and prayed without avail. And the Voice spoke to him:

"Francis, if you had faith as big as a mustard seed, you would tell that mountain to disappear, and it would do so."

"What mountain, Lord?"

"The mountain of temptation."

"My Lord," he said, weeping, "be it granted to me according to thy word!" And the temptation disappeared, and he could dwell again in peace and serenity.

The coming and going of the Great Temptation are not to be securely dated and fitted into a psychological progress. But at some time in these years his spirit was lightened; in true humility he accepted the behest of the men in command. With Brothers Leo and Bonizzo he returned to Fonte Colombo, to make an inoffensive version of his Second Rule.

He was listless even in this set task. His work was mostly excision. He eliminated all but a few of the biblical citations that had constituted over half of the First Rule. He cut the requirements that the newer recruits to the order found so burdensome. In disregard of Christ's command to his apostles, he allowed his friars to wear shoes and to possess two tunics in place of one. He dropped the requirement of manual labor, lest it interfere with the spirit of prayer and devotion of which labor is the mere servant. He no longer forbade the ownership of books, although he stipulated that illiterate friars should make no effort to learn to read. A provision in the First Rule permitting the brothers to denounce unworthy masters ("ministers") was stricken out. The requirement of poverty was considerably eased, with the omission of the biblical injunction that disciples carry nothing on their way. The resulting document was brief — only about two thousand words — and chilly. It is a legal, impersonal constitution. Says the learned Omer Englebert: "It is a canonical text to be interpreted by jurists — a series of prescriptions and prohibitions for them to decide whether they oblige *sub gravi* or *sub levi* (seriously or lightly) and in which they would later find matter for twenty-seven mortal sins." And Paul Sabatier, comparing the two rules, says in summary: "The free impulse of love has become an act of submission, by which life eternal will be earned."

Nevertheless the Second Rule was better than no rule at all, as Francis recognized. He went to Rome in the latter part of 1223, to lobby for the official acceptance of the rule. He was warmly welcomed by the cardinals, by the pope himself, by Giacoma dei Settesoli. He was lodged splendidly in a private tower on the great estate of Cardinal Brancaleoni. He was embarrassed by such magnificence; it seemed like an infidelity to Lady Poverty. And on his first night there he was assailed by horrible demons, who beat him black and blue. He called his companion, and said: "If the demons, whose power is only that accorded them by divine Providence, have attacked me so savagely, it is because my entertainment at the court of the great sets a bad example. If my brothers, who live in poor little refuges, learn that I am associating with cardinals, they may think that I am immersed in worldly concerns, wallowing in luxury, and undone by honors. A man whose business is to set an example for others should flee palaces and dwell humbly in humble quarters in the midst of the humble in order to strengthen them, in their wretchedness, by sharing it."

Despite the triple recurrence of the word "humble" this does not seem a very humble remark. A man who is convinced that his business is to set an example for others runs the risk of losing his honesty of purpose in spiritual pride. One would think that his business should be rather following the great example than posing before others.

Francis in person handed the text of the new rule to Pope Honorius, insisting, in a burst of his old self-confidence, that the words were not his own, but had been dictated by God.

The pope signed the Second Rule on 29 November, thus making it canonical law. Perhaps he recalled that his first act in office had been to authorize the plenary indulgence, or Great Pardon, of the Portiuncula, in 1216.

Francis immediately turned north to the Vale of Rieti, which he had come to love dearly. In the quiet caves were no jangling voices, no complaints to be settled, troubles to be resolved. Here one could be out of time, out of touch with men, intimate only with God.

Christmas was at hand, the festival best beloved by Francis. Tommaso da Celano tells us that he celebrated the day beyond all others in the year, for then Baby Jesus proved his humanity, sucking his mother's milk, by divine condescension. "The name of Jesus was like honey on his lips." One year when Christmas fell on a Friday the question was propounded: do we abstain from meat or do we not? Francis cried out that it was a sin to fast on Christ's birthday; even the oxen and the asses should receive a double ration of oats and hay on that blessed day. He made the pains of the Holy Mother his own. When a brother depicted, at table, her destitution, he rose, shaking with sobs, to finish his scraps of bread on the floor.

Before leaving Rome, Francis asked and received the pope's permission to reenact the Christmas drama. Such authorization was necessary, for as recently as 1207 Innocent III had forbidden the representation of theatrical games, *ludi theatrales,* in churches. The ban suggests that such performances were increasing in popularity.

Arriving in Rieti a fortnight before Christmas, Francis looked up a friend, both noble and pious, who owned a part of the mountain wall, ten miles from Rieti, near the village of Greccio. Here was a hermit's cave, and below it a level space, which seems today manifestly designed for parking. Francis proposed to his friend that he lend the area for a Christmas midnight mass, with an introductory pageant. The friend took fire at Francis's words: "I want to evoke the memory of the child born in Bethlehem with all the sufferings he endured in his childhood. I want to see him with the eyes of the flesh, just as he was, lying in a manger and sleeping on the hay between an ox and an ass." The whole village set to work, clearing the glade, cutting torches and making candles. The actors, including the ox and the ass, learned their parts. Says Tommaso da Celano:

> Simplicity was in full honor there; it was the triumph of poverty, humility's best lesson. Greccio had become a new Bethlehem. Night was turned into day, as delightfully for animals as for men. The woods reverberated with holy songs, and the mountain returned them as joyous echos. The brothers sang the praise of God, and the night passed in joy. The saint stood vigil before the cradle, broken with emotion and unspeakable joy. Finally the mass was celebrated with the manger as altar, and the celebrant priest felt such consolation as he had never before known. Francis, wearing his deacon's dalmatic, sang the Gospel with his loud voice. . . . Then he preached to the people and found words sweet as

honey with which to speak of the poor little king and of the small town of Bethlehem. Speaking of Christ Jesus, he called him tenderly "Bethlehem's baby," and he prolonged in utterance this "Bethlehem," like a lamb's bleating, and all his love seemed to emerge from his lips. And when he said "Jesus," or "Bethlehem's baby," he passed his tongue over his lips as if to savor the sweetness of these words.

This moving ceremony marks the beginning of the *presepio,* the *crèche,* the Christmas crib, in the Christian world. It is true that scholars have seen its origins in the liturgical dramas in France, and true that models of the Nativity had been displayed in great Roman churches. Nevertheless, in that midnight mass of 1223 Francis set the precedent and form for the Christmas cribs that delight the faithful, and the unfaithful, in our cities and homes today. Further, he stimulated, if he did not invent, the cult of the baby in religion. With the ancients, the divine infant was a mere grotesque, like Hercules the snake-strangler, like Romulus and Remus the wolf's foster cubs, like lewd Cupid. Child gods in eastern religions are rare indeed; are there any beside the baby Buddha? But the infant Jesus remains our dearest deity, figuring our longing for innocence, simplicity.

After the famous Christmas of 1223, Francis retired to the hermitage of Greccio, high in the cloven wall. There you may see the grotto of the first *presepio,* and the boulder on which the manger-altar was laid, and the stone bed on which the saint slept, and the tiny church and rough dormitory of the thirteenth century, and an almost contemporary fresco of Francis wiping his wounded eye. Thence one passes to the handsome modern church with a *presepio* of life-size figures. And if your trip is well planned, you may arrive on Christmas Eve, to join the throng that climbs the mountainside, candle in hand, to kneel with Saint Francis in celebration of the perpetual miracle.

ELEVEN

The Stigmata

FRANCIS REMAINED in the Greccio retreat through the Lenten season of 1224. He was grieved to note a relaxation of devotional fervor among the brothers. It seems that spirituality displays a tendency to yield to gravitational forces. As Easter approached the companions planned a surprise — a fine dinner in celebration of the Resurrection and in honor of their distinguished guest. How little they understood him and the old ideals of his order! Francis got wind of the goings-on, peeked into the refectory, and saw there a table set with a cloth and glasses! He tiptoed away, hunted down a poor pilgrim and borrowed his staff and battered hat. The dinner hour came, and the friars, who had been instructed never to wait for the Master, set eagerly to the breaking of the Lenten fast. Then came a knock at the door, and a bedraggled creature whined: "For the love of God, give alms to a poor sick pilgrim!" The visiting minister, who of course recognized him, replied: "Brother, we too are poor, and as we are numerous we need the victuals that men give us. But, for the love of God whom you have invoked, enter, and we shall give you a share of the alms that the Lord has granted us." He entered; the minister handed his own bowl with his half-finished portion and a piece of bread to the newcomer, who took the proffered gift and sat on the floor near the fire to eat. "When I saw this rich and sumptuous spread," he said, "I thought this was hardly the table of poor religious begging from door to door. We should cultivate humility and poverty more than other religious, for that is the life to which we have been summoned, and we have promised to follow it before God and men. Now, I think, I am seated as a Friar Minor should be." And all were covered with confusion, and many wept.

The refectory, scene of this little drama, remains in its primitive simplicity at the Greccio hermitage.

Shortly afterward, Francis went to the Portiuncula, to attend the general chapter held at Pentecost. And in August, restless again, he determined to visit his order's retreat at Mount La Verna.

La Verna — often written Alverna — stands next only to Assisi as a Franciscan shrine. Even to the skeptical its history seems to have been directed by destiny. It is an Apennine summit, a heap of tumbled rock, an outcrop of Mount Penna, standing about three thousand feet above the Casentino valley. It is very beautiful and somewhat terrifying. It has been called an altar raised in the very heart of central Italy; and Saint Teresa of Avila — who did not, however, see it — termed it the great castle of the soul. In winter it shows another aspect; the snow whips level from the north; the trees bend and groan; the rock crevices howl and lament. "It's only the wind," say reasonable visitors; but many have recognized the voices of demons.

La Verna came into the possession of the Franciscan order in May 1213, when the missionary work was just beginning. The *Little Flowers* tells the story. Francis and Brother Leo, spreading the Word through the Marches, came to the village of San Leo, near San Marino. About the picturesque castle of Montefeltro clustered a melee of horses, squires, and grooms. The two evangelists learned that one of the counts of Montefeltro had just been dubbed knight, and that a grand banquet was soon to be served. The saint then said to the brother: "Let's go up and join the party, for with God's help we may do some spiritual good."

So the two entered the castle courtyard, and Francis climbed on a low wall and began to preach. He commanded attention; and one by one all fell silent. He took as his text a couplet from the vernacular — from an earthy love song, in fact:

> *Such are the blessings I foresee*
> *That every pain is joy to me.*

He told of the sufferings and martyrdoms of the apostles, and of the penances and tribulations of holy virgins and other saints, and everyone listened spellbound, as to an angel of God, with no thought for the chilling banquet. We are not told the responses of the newly knighted count of Montefeltro, finding himself eclipsed by the ragged preacher.

Now it chanced that one of the guests was a Count Orlando, rich and noble, whose castle stood in Chiusi, in a fold of the Apennines, below Mount Penna. He had heard stories of Francis and was much stirred by his impromptu sermon. He asked for a private interview, to discuss his soul's welfare. The interview brought Count Orlando much solace and at its end he remarked: "I own, just over the Tuscan border, a mountain called La Verna, very fit for the practice of piety. It is very solitary, well forested, just the thing for one who might want to do penance in a place outside of the world, or for someone who wants only a hermit's life. If you like it, I shall gladly give it to you and your companions, for the good of my soul." Francis's curiosity was aroused. On returning to the Portiuncula he sent two of the comrades to Count Orlando, who deputed fifty horsemen to guide the friars and protect them from wolves. The scouts found the site uplifting and soothing, very proper for contemplation and meditation, though clearly worthless for agriculture. They built a rude hut out of branches for Francis, and returned to recommend the acceptance of Count Orlando's offer. This Francis granted, with a sophistical speech insisting on fidelity to holy poverty but recommending nonetheless acquisition of the property. Since the only deed was an oral promise, the taint of ownership was avoided.

In the following years La Verna was occasionally used as a retreat for the friars. Francis may have visited it in 1215 or another year, but it is more likely that he never saw the scene of his momentous spiritual drama until 1224. After the Pentecostal chapter meeting of that year, his health seems to have markedly improved; he determined to make the eighty-mile journey on foot to the mountaintop. He took with him five companions, his closest friends in the order — Masseo, Angelo Tancredi, Leo, Rufino, and Illuminato.

It was like old times, to be out on the familiar roads of Umbria again, empty-handed, trusting to God's favor for food and shelter. But Francis soon found that time and illness and self-castigation had shaken him sorely and had dimmed the joys of the open road. On the second night out the brothers took refuge in a half-ruined church. While the others slept, Francis prayed. This was apparently a mistake, for he was attacked by a horde of ferocious demons, who dragged him to and fro on the floor and showered him with abuse, but they could not bend him. In the morning he was so shattered and undone that he could scarcely proceed. The companions persuaded a kindly peasant to lend his ass for the remainder of the journey. On the way the peasant complained bitterly of thirst, and Francis, by prayer, caused a stream of water to burst forth from the dry rocks. This scene is the theme of one of Giotto's frescoes in the Upper Church of the Assisi basilica.

"And as they approached the base of the crowning rock of La Verna," says the *Little Flowers*, "it pleased Saint Francis to rest a while under an oak, which is still there." No, it is no longer there; when at length it died the Chapel of the Birds replaced it.

And there assembled a great throng of birds of various kinds, expressing by singing and beating their wings their great joy and delight. And they so clustered about Saint Francis that some settled on his head, shoulders, and arms, others on his breast and others around his feet. At this sight his companions and the peasant were amazed, and Saint Francis, overjoyed, said: "I think, dear Brothers, that our Lord Jesus Christ wants us to live on this solitary mountain, since our brothers and sisters the birds show so much joy at our coming."

Soon Count Orlando rode up from his castle in the valley with a troop of men bearing food and useful supplies. He set the men to work building temporary lodgings and a rude chapel. Then Francis preached a little sermon in praise of poverty, concluding: "Since I recognize that my death is near at hand I intend to live in solitude, to seek God's presence and bewail my sins before Him. Brother Leo will bring me a little bread and water when he pleases. On no account permit any secular person to come near me." So saying, he retired to his cell, erected under a solitary beech tree. The presumed site is marked today by a sixteenth-century chapel.

Francis's escape into a private world naturally roused the curiosity of the five companions. Leo, presuming on old intimacy, spied on the Master, and was rewarded by seeing him frequently levitated to a height of about twenty feet, sometimes to the treetops, and once nearly out of sight.*

Francis was uncomfortable at being watched by Leo. He looked for a more secure retreat, and found it on a ledge overhanging a precipice. This could be reached only by means of a log bridging a deep gap. There the brothers erected a hut of reeds. Francis ordered Leo to visit him

---

* Most miracles can be explained away, as exaggerations or variations of familiar reality. But levitation is absolute; it must be exactly true or totally false. I do not believe Brother Leo's story; in fact, I do not believe he ever told the story. I have omitted from this book a vast number of miracles attributed to Saint Francis — astounding cures, predictions, multiplication of foods — because they seem readily explicable by natural means or by man's mythmaking impulse. They fit within my conspectus of the world's behavior. Thus I judge between true and false, accepting this, rejecting that. But by what right do I assume the privilege of judgment? May not a higher court quash my judgment and question my right to make it? Certainly; and in the present instance the reader is the highest terrestrial court of appeal.

twice a day, once bringing water, and once, at midnight, to recite matins with him.

But Francis was not quite alone. An angel provided celestial music. The devil was a constant visitor, playing a comic role of discomfiture and frustration. And a falcon that nested nearby took Francis under his special care, coming regularly at midnight to wake him for matins, by beating his wings against the hut. However, if Francis was very tired or ill, the falcon would allow him a couple of extra hours for sleep, evidently with the connivance of Brother Leo. In the morning the falcon was joined by a chorus of various birds. Each in turn would stand forth, sing a solo, and politely yield place to another chorister.

Francis did not cling to his ledge; he wandered in the woods, and would often retreat to a cave included in the present structures of La Verna. It is a horrid dismal hole, filled with huge dripping rocks, pervaded with a perpetual chill. We are shown a boulder where Francis came to pray, occasionally stretching out on that wet bed of stone. How could the sick man have survived?

The day of the Assumption, 15 August, approached. Francis determined to undertake a more rigorous fast than was his wont until Michaelmas, 29 September. His extreme sufferings, in flesh and spirit, he attributed to the malice of the devil, not to his own outrages to Brother Ass. Visions of holiness as well as of evil visited him. He told Brother Leo that he had learned in revelation that something marvelous was going to happen soon at La Verna. He had Leo seek the explanation by consulting his missal; at each trial the book fell open to the Passion of Christ. Thus, said Leo afterwards, Francis was assured that as he had followed the Savior in all the acts of His life he was suffered to follow and imitate Him in all the afflictions and pains of His Passion. He rejoiced that this privilege was to be his.

He was granted his apotheosis an hour before dawn on 14 September 1224, a holy day in the Franciscan calendar. It was the feast of the Exaltation of the Cross. Francis lay in one of the rocky interstices of the mountain caves. The spot is now the Chapel of the Stigmata. As Brother Leo reported, Francis prayed and was assured that God would permit him to share His Son's sufferings.

> And the fervor of his devotion increased so much that he totally transformed himself into Him who let himself be crucified through abundance of love. . . . Suddenly appeared to him a seraph with six wings, bearing enfolded in them a very beautiful image of a crucified man, his hands and feet outflung as on a cross, with features clearly resembling those of Lord Jesus. Two wings covered the seraph's head; two, descending to his feet, veiled the rest of his body; the other two were unfolded for flight.

Francis understood that this vision was vouchsafed him to show that he was to be utterly transformed into the likeness of the crucified Christ, not by the torture of his body but by love inflaming his soul. At the moment of his vision a weird light illumined the mountain, frightening some benighted shepherds and providing one more parallel with the Christ story.

Then Christ himself appeared in the grotto, and spoke to Francis certain secret, sublime words, which, of course, were never revealed. The saintly adept had won to the last, the supreme stage of the Mystic Way, the stage of union, when the supplicant is merged into the long-sought Paraclete, God of God, Light of Light, Very God of Very God. The bliss, foretaste of heaven, overwhelms the searcher as he himself becomes a part of God, becomes God.

The vision faded; and Francis discovered on his hands and feet the marks of nails, and on his right side a blood-dripping wound, such as he had just seen in vision.

> His hands and feet seemed to be pierced in the middle by nails, whose heads, protruding out of the flesh, were in the palms of the hands and on the upper part of the feet, while the points emerged from the back of the hands and the soles of the feet. They seemed to be bent back, clinched, so that one could easily have passed a finger, as in a ring, under the bent part, which came completely out of the flesh. The heads of the nails were black and round. Similarly, on his right side appeared the wound of a lance thrust, not scabbed but red and bloody. Afterwards blood often dripped from the holy breast of Saint Francis, staining his robe and his drawers. Thus when his comrades noticed — he had told them nothing — that he kept his hands and feet covered and that he could not put his feet to the ground, and that when they washed his gown and drawers for him they found them all bloody, they were certain that he had manifestly imprinted on his hands and feet and even on his side the image and resemblance of the crucified Christ.

Since the presence of the stigmata could hardly be dissembled, Francis decided to acknowledge them, for the edification of his close friends and followers. He exhibited them first to Leo, who acted as his nurse and bathed the oozing wound in the side. Saint Bonaventure says that more than fifty, among them Pope Alexander IV, were privileged to see and touch the holy imprints. But Francis was shy of revealing his sweet torture to the general. He kept his hands and feet bandaged, and hid himself to wash his wounds. When someone sought to kiss his hands he would extend only the tips of his fingers, or his sleeve. A comrade, surprising him and perceiving the stigmata on his feet, said: "What's this, brother?" and received the ungracious reply: "Mind your own business." The wounds were painful; his side, constantly oozing blood, was horrible to tender observers. He wore gloves and soft woolen moccasins, with a leather patch on the sole to shield the tortured foot from the rough wool. A pair of socks made for him by Santa Chiara herself is displayed in her Assisi church.

We approach now the central, the difficult problem. What, actually, were the stigmata? How, if at all, can we accord them with our concept of the physical world? Can we even describe them in acceptable terms?

Look to the history of stigmatization. The idea, and the use of the word, go back to Saint Paul: "I bear in my body the marks (*stigmata*) of the Lord Jesus." But clearly the apostle is using the word figuratively, without reference to the crucifixion wounds. Thenceforward it occurred to no one, not even to Deity, to implant the wounds on a living human body, until the time of Francis. The *Catholic Encyclopedia* tells us that Blessed Mary of Oignies, who died in 1213, reproduced on her own body the marks of Christ's Passion; but apparently these marks were mere centers of tenderness and pain. Father Herbert Thurston, S.J., in his *Physical Phenomena of Mysticism*, reports a stigmatic who was brought before the Council at Canterbury in 1222, two years before

Francis's experience. He bore the five wounds of the crucifixion, with perforated hands and feet. Father Thurston concludes that the wounds were self-inflicted, and that the young man was probably mad. He called himself Jesus, and was accompanied by a female disciple, who assumed the name of Mary, Christ's mother. To prove his sanctity he allowed himself to be crucified. Far from convincing the judges of his deification, he and his follower were condemned to be walled up until Nature should release them. A hermaphrodite suffered the same punishment.

We can hardly accept these cases — and some others less decisive — as establishing an "influence," or setting a precedent for Francis to follow consciously. They offer no traceable connection; they occurred at a great distance, and lack the Franciscan mystical spirit. All contemporary writers regarded Francis's stigmatization as something unique, unheard of. But the publicity attending his spiritual adventure inspired a swarm of imitators, created a vogue. A modern investigator turned up 31 cases by the end of the thirteenth century, 22 in the fourteenth, 25 in the fifteenth — 321 in all, before 1894. Of these 40 were men, 281 women. All modern critics agree that the investigator was too lenient in admitting doubtful or insufficiently documented examples; but on the other hand there were probably many obscure cases that were never documented at all.

The phenomenon still occurs. There was the case of Louise Lateau in Belgium (1850–1883), who developed not only the five wounds but also a ring of thorn pricks around her head. Bloody blisters appeared every Friday, and burst during the day. Her case was exhaustively examined by the Royal Academy of Belgium, which concluded that the facts were genuine, that no fraud was involved; but it could offer no rational explanation. There was Theresa Neumann of Konnersreuth in Bavaria, who first displayed the stigmata on Good Friday of 1926. She was a visionary, possessed of a dual or multiple personality. There is Padre Pio, a Capuchin friar of Foggia, who was apparently still living in 1955. The wound in his side is said to have yielded a cupful of blood daily. There was a case in Montreal, some fifty years ago. The eminent physician Jonathan Campbell Meakins, physician-in-chief of the Royal Victoria Hospital and president of the American College of Physicians, told me that he examined the stigmatized woman in the hospital and could find no material explanation of her state. There were no doubt others, protected from reporters and photographers by families unwilling to divulge secrets, whether alarming or precious.

How then should we regard Francis's stigmata, commonly taken to be the convincing evidence of his saintliness, God's imprimatur?

Remember that in all his adult life Francis had practiced the imitation of Christ. His prayers and praises were not merely homage to his Master, but efforts for identification with Him. Saint Bonaventure recognized this clearly: "Our Man of God understood that after imitating Christ's deeds in his life, he should resemble Him still further in the afflictions and sufferings of His Passion before quitting the world." He would imitate his Master even to the point of rivaling with Him. It was not enough for Francis to be Christlike — he would be Christ.

One's interpretation of the stigmata must depend

largely on one's conception of Francis, as, contrariwise, one's conclusions about the stigmata help to determine one's conception of him.

I recognize five coherent explanations of the stigmata.

1. They were an authentic miracle. "But," you will say, "I deny all miracles. A miracle is by definition a violation of natural law. The smallest of miracles — say the cure of an actually incurable disease — requires the abolition of cause and effect, and hence, eventually, the shattering of all the sequences of world order, the destruction of the solar system, if not, indeed, of the universe. There is no use alleging eyewitnesses and testimonies. I agree with Diderot, and I think Hume, who said that if a thousand witnesses swear to the truth of an impossibility, the witnesses are mistaken."

Thereto another may object: "You are confusing the impossible with the merely unusual. Modern physics is reluctant to speak of laws, regarding old-fashioned laws rather as habits, which may be momentarily abrogated. The behavior of particles may, in one out of an infinite number of cases, suddenly turn eccentric. The concept of cause and effect is called in question; the Principle of Indeterminacy rules. Accept that God created the universe; surely it is no harder for Him to make a minute variation than to make a first creation. As for miracles, everything is a miracle, a grain of desert sand, a drop of sea water, is a miracle. Did you ever watch a fat green pupa transform itself into a butterfly and flutter miraculously away? Fear not; believe that the stigmata were miraculously conferred on Francis and perhaps on certain others, and you have the authority of the Church behind you, and the attestation of numberless wise men, who have learned more than you ever will about divine action on the human spirit.

2. Not at all. Since there are no miracles, there were no stigmata. It was all a trick. Francis obtained Brother Leo's testimony by his dominating, perhaps hypnotic, power; thenceforth he was careful to keep his hands, feet, and side hidden. As for the recognition of the stigmata after his death, obviously Brother Elias or another slipped into the Portiuncula church and faked the wounds on his exposed body.

There are a number of things wrong with this solution, of which the chief is the character of Francis. Men reveal themselves by consistency of behavior; the charlatan never completely hides his charlatanism. But Francis was no charlatan, and the supposition that he would make a charlatan's game out of his dealings with his Savior is incredible. Also incredible is the presumption that the faithful followers would have united in an enormous fraud to promote the worldly welfare of the order. And as for the supposed fabrication of postmortem evidence, his brothers watched the night, chanting psalms, by his bier, and the city authorities posted armed guards around it, for fear that the Perugians would steal the precious relic. There was no opportunity for a pious fraud.

No, the stigmatization was not the product of conscious trickery. The rewards were inconsequential, the procedures difficult and painful, the deception hard to sustain. Above all, the motive alleged is insufficient, as is the evidence adduced.

3. The cause may be sought in abnormal neurotic or psychotic behavior. The wounds were self-inflicted, in accesses of ecstasy or of dementia. There are a number of such cases in the history of stigmatization. I have men-

tioned the man who had himself crucified in Canterbury, in 1222. Gabriel Sagard, a Recollect, or rigorous Franciscan, came out to Canada to convert the Indians in 1623. He tells of a comrade in his French monastery who crucified himself in his cell and nearly died. The most sensational example is that of Matteo Lovat, a village shoemaker from Casale, near Venice, in the early part of the nineteenth century. To combat lust he removed his testicles and tossed them out the window to the surprised villagers. When he recovered, he constructed a cross from his bedframe with a rigging of ropes to support his body. He stripped, put on a crown of thorns, and with the utmost ingenuity nailed himself to the cross.

But this is mere insanity, the grotesque exaggeration of piety! It recalls the caperings of the eunuch priests of Baal, scarifying themselves with knives to appease a bloodthirsty god. Francis's wounds were not gashes inflicted in frenzy. And he was not insane. An outsider in his world, if you like; an eccentric in the very excesses of his faith; a man possessed by his abounding love for his Maker; a seer of visions, of course. But he was always rational, more rational than the run of men. If this is insanity we must doubt our own sanity.

4. We must look further. Perhaps the clue lies not with the stigmatized sufferer but with the reporters. The story as we have it is the exaggeration of an acceptable fact. We all know how a story develops in the telling, as each reteller pulls a little toward himself, softens a little the discrepancies and awkwardnesses of his story. Certainly Francis had an hour of mystic rapture, and found himself with telltale marks, possibly self-inflicted, perhaps the product of much rubbing and chafing in ecstatic prayer. So much we may accept. But is it credible that the

marks continued unaltered, the wound in the side open, for two years? Are we to believe the story of an incredulous haughty knight who, reenacting Saint Thomas the Doubter, refused to believe in the wounds unless he could touch; so he was permitted to move the excrescent nails and feel the wound in Francis's side? Thereafter he was a constant witness to their reality, and at the same time a supporter of the identification of Francis with Jesus. In our turn we may doubt the doubter. We may boggle too over Leo's statement that Francis generated from his own flesh flexible, curved, nail-like rings, through which one could pass a finger. We may find belief easier if we are permitted to make some subtractions, of what we take to be legendary accretions. But there lies our difficulty. Who draws the line between legend and reality? That distinction depends only on the belief, or the whim, of the reader.

At least, no alleged miracle has been better observed and attested than that of Francis. Dismiss, if you like, those aspects of the story that sound like pious additions or editorial revisions; it remains clear that something occurred in the cell at La Verna, something outside our common experience, something not to be satisfactorily explained by most of the solutions proposed by believers and unbelievers.

5. If we accept, then, that the stigmata were not imposed from without, whether by miracle or human subterfuge, but that they emerged from within, we find ourselves in the murky realm of the subconscious. This is no new-discovered land. Petrarch, writing in 1367 a letter on the power of the imagination, attributes the imposition of the stigmata to imagination. He says: "Saint Francis's meditation on Christ's death was so constant and

forceful that he transferred it for long to his own mind. He felt himself nailed to the cross with his Master, and finally his pious imagination transplanted the marks from his mind to actuality in his body." Petrarch skips lightly over the question of how the imagination may transplant marks from the mind to actuality; the medieval man had no difficulty in believing in the interaction of mind and body.

There are words for the phenomenon of the stigmata — autosuggestion of the hysteric type, says the Jesuit Father Thurston, in a book valuable but now outdated. A "traumatic neurosis" might be an acceptable term. But the words do not help us much. Psychiatrists and psychoanalysts present many cases of physical traumata provoked by mental causes. Father Thurston himself records that at the Paris Salpétrière hospital patterns and inscriptions have been produced on subjects' flesh by mere suggestion.

I am too ignorant and too timid to attempt an excursion into the dark cellars of the subconscious. But I suspect that here lies the clue to the nature of the stigmata, and perhaps to the troubles and tortures and glories of Francis of Assisi. The material lies at hand — his rivalry with his father and with his brother; and the shackling of the youth by his father and his unshackling by his mother — there is a symbol for you. And Francis's painful sense of inferiority, his sexual torment, his identification with Jesus, his obsession with self-stripping — everything is ready to hand for the psychological detective. It is a subject awaiting an author.

We return to Francis on the summit of La Verna. On 29 September, Michaelmas, his rigorous fast ended. The nights had turned chill, bringing a foretaste of winter.

Francis assembled his little party for the return to the lowlands. As he could not walk on his wounded feet, he obtained a donkey, that humble, comic, sanctified bearer of divinity. He paused in a number of towns and villages, to receive popular acclaim and to perform miraculous cures. And so he came once more to the haven of the Portiuncula.

TWELVE

The Song of the Creatures

THE CHRONOLOGY of Francis's last two years is a matter of dispute, compounded of honest doubt and the furious local patriotism of antiquarians. The evidence has been scrupulously examined by Father Ignatius Brady, O.F.M., and Raphael Brown, in their edition of Omer Englebert's *Saint Francis of Assisi,* and I accept their reconstruction of the order of events gratefully and without cavil.

In October 1224 Francis, bearing the stigmata, descended from La Verna to the Portiuncula. He rested only briefly. During the following winter and spring, despite his pains, he undertook donkey-borne tours of Umbria, stopping sometimes to preach in three or four villages in a single day. He would not heed the adjurations of his companions to consult a doctor — probably a good thing. In March 1225 he paid a visit to Chiara at San Damiano. While there he was attacked by an acute eye trouble, so severe that he could hardly be moved. It was decided that he would be better off at San Damiano than in the Portiuncula, which lies in a damp, foggy valley. A cell of reed mats was constructed for him against, or more likely within, the little house accommodating the chaplain and two lay workers, questing brothers, who did the outdoor work and collected alms and groceries for the sisters. We are sometimes told by modern writers that Francis was tenderly nursed by Chiara. But there is something peculiar about this. San Damiano had been put under a strict papal enclosure by Honorius III in 1218, and the two saints could properly have communicated only through a grilled window. This Pyramus-and-Thisbe situation was a torturing one for both; but maybe Francis in his weakness and Chiara in her determination defied the pope and his closures.

To add to Francis's sufferings, his cell was ridden with field mice. These would run over his body and filch his food from under his groping fingers. He took the mice to be the devil's minions; he never uttered any praise of mice or claimed any brotherhood with them. He prayed to be delivered from the creatures, and received from Heaven only the answer that he should cease complaining, that the greatest of treasures was reserved for him, the treasure of salvation to eternal life.

And now, stricken as he was, he revealed a new Francis, Francis the poet. He had of course composed minstrel songs and *vers d'occasion,* light verse for light moments. Now he attempted a serious poem expressing his love for the beautiful world and its inhabitants, his praise of all the loveliness fading before his stricken eyes. He initiated the great course of Italian poetic literature. Before him Italy could show a vernacular poetic school only in half-foreign Sicily. His poem stands first in every Italian anthology. He was the forerunner of Dante, Petrarch, Leopardi, Montale . . .

His poem is the "Cantico di Frate Sole," "Canticle of Brother Sun," commonly known in English as "The Song of the Creatures." It begins:

Altissimo onnipotente bon Signore,
tue so le laudi li gloria e l'onore e onne benedizione . . .

Most high and most holy, most powerful Lord,
Whom with honor and blessing and praise we acclaim,
No man can be worthy to utter the word,
The Name of thy Name!

To Thee and thy creatures we proffer our praise:
To our brother the Sun in the heavens ashine,
Who brings us the beauty and joy of our days,
Thy emblem and sign.

We praise thee, O Lord, for our sister the moon,
For the stars of the night shining sweetly together,
For our brother the wind, for the bright of the noon,
For all of thy weather.

For our sister the water, so humble and chaste,
For beautiful fire, with his perilous powers,
For our mother the earth, who holds us embraced,
Who delights us with flowers.

"The Song of the Creatures" has been called a nature poem, animated by a pantheistic spirit. It is that indeed, but Francis would have protested that he was no pantheist. He would have called himself a humble celebrant of God's bounty in providing man with beauty and wonder; his poem was a religious poem. The world was not God, though it was godlike, a manifestation of God, responding gratefully to its Creator. Tommaso da Celano was in the right of it; he wrote:

> In every work, Saint Francis admired the Workman; he credited the Creator with all the qualities he discovered in every creature. He rejoiced in all the works emerging from the hand of God; and, taking his start from this joyous spectacle, he found his way to Him who is the cause, principle, and life of the universe. In contemplating a beautiful object, he could contemplate the perfect beauty.

Thus Francis, though unlearned, had his own coherent esthetic theory.

For most moderns, devout worshipers or not, Francis represents the appreciation and love of nature, of the physical world, of mere wonderful earth and fire and water. This was one of Francis's discoveries, revelations. Of course the men of the early Middle Age recognized and loved natural beauty, flowers and birdsong and graceful animals and sweet faces. But in their poems and paintings they conventionalized beauty, representing it in ever-recurrent forms. In their lyric poems the year was perpetually maytime, with unnamed flowers blooming and unspecified birds caroling. Their paintings, still rigidly Byzantine, showed backgrounds always of formalized rocks and chasms. Francis's nature was a reality, alive, diverse, conscious of its Creator and responsive to Him. It was observed in love, and celebrated with joy.

At San Damiano, then, he dictated "The Song of the Creatures," with an accompanying melody, which has been lost. Chiara was certainly one of the first to hear it. He then did nothing but sing his canticle for a week. He proposed to send a group of friars from village to village, preaching; and after the sermon they would all chant his poem. He desired further to recruit a brilliant preacher (Anthony of Padua?) to tour the great churches, with a choir of friars led by Fra Pacifico, the former King of Poetry; and all would intone his canticle. Francis was not devoid of author's vanity.

Now it happened that at this time Francis's old friend and patron, Bishop Guido of Assisi, was enjoying a bitter quarrel with the mayor, Oportulo. The mayor had fined some of the bishop's adherents; the bishop excommunicated the mayor; the mayor forbade all citizens to speak to the bishop, to deal with him or to bring him food. Each party imposed sanctions, we should say today; and sanctions had no more effect then than now. Francis grieved that his Christian friends should so yield to un-Christian behavior. He summoned one of the brothers and said: "Go to see the mayor and tell him from me to proceed to the bishop's palace with the notables of the commune." (He took as a matter of course his right to command the masters of Church and state.) Then he ordered the brothers to join the assemblage and at the right moment to demand silence and to sing his canticle in praise of the Lord for all His creatures; and at the end to add this stanza:

> We praise Thee for those who for thy sake forgive,
>   Whom sorrow and sickness will never cast down,
> Who in peace persevering will resolute live;
>   They shall merit Thy crown.

The praise was directed significantly at the quarreling officials, but surely Francis was thinking of his own fate. The party duly assembled and the stanza of pardon was sung. The mayor clasped his hands as for the reading of the Gospel, and he wept abundantly. And he proclaimed: "Not only do I pardon the bishop, whom I must recognize as my master, but I would pardon the murderer of my brother or of my son!" He knelt and begged the bishop for forgiveness. The bishop raised him up, saying: "My office requires humility, but I am testy-tempered by nature; you must pardon me." So both embraced and exchanged the kiss of peace, with much tenderness and affection.

The incident illustrates the power of Christian love, and also Francis's use of love to persuade and command. Love is the clue to Francis. He loved all the aspects of the external world, from sun, moon, earth, fire and water to insects and to stones in the road. Especially he loved living creatures, and of them especially birds. Best of the birds, to him, were the cowled larks, earth-colored like monks, and humble, but such sweet singers! The larks returned his love. On the night before his death a great multitude came and wheeled above his roof, singing their farewell. One may remember his warm reception by the birds of La Verna. On another occasion a swarm of birds — wood pigeons, crows, rooks — assembled on a tree to hear his sermon, and at the end bowed their heads reverently down; and again a brawling band of swallows fell silent at his command. He tamed many birds for pets, or rather companions — his familiar hawk at La Verna, a loving moorhen, a family of robins, one of whom suffered death as penalty for gluttony, a pheasant who followed him like a dog. The birds in Giotto's fresco are identified as goldfinches, quail, sparrows, and pigeons. Francis proposed even that the state should undertake to throw grain for the birds on the roads every Christmas, as a present. There was a pet crow who went begging for the brothers, and who, at Francis's passing, came to die on his grave.

How different was the attitude of Francis's rival, Saint Dominic! Preaching in a nunnery, he was disturbed by an importunate sparrow, obviously the devil. He seized the bird and plucked off his feathers one by one, amid the loud laughter of the sisters. He then threw the bird out to seek a more gullible victim.

Only less than birds Francis loved the beasts. He was always moved by the beauty of innocent lambs, symbolic of his Savior's charges. Once, at Greccio, a brother brought him a hare taken in a snare. Said Francis: "Come here, little brother hare. Why did you let yourself get caught?" The hare ran to Francis and buried his head in the saintly breast. Francis caressed him for a time, then set him free; but he would merely come bounding back to his rescuer, who finally had him carried to the forest to get lost. On the other hand, Francis did not extend his tender love to the poor familiar ass, which must be forever ill fed and well beaten to its duty, like the human body. And he never had a kind word for field mice.

One of the most celebrated, and least convincing, of the animal stories is that of the wolf of Gubbio. A huge and terrible wolf appeared in the neighborhood, and devoured both animals and men, so that countrymen armed themselves as if going out to battle. Therefore Francis, putting all his trust in God, issued forth to overcome him. The dreadful beast sprang ravening at the presumptuous human, and Francis made the sign of the holy cross upon him; whereat the wolf closed his jaws and lay down humbly. Francis reproved Brother Wolf for his misdeeds, and promised him that if he would reform no man or dog would mistreat him. Brother Wolf wagged his tail, twitched his ears, and bowed his head in acquiescence. So the pact was made; and the wolf lifted up his right paw and laid it gently in Francis's hand. The wolf lived for two more years in Gubbio, visiting people's houses freely, doing no hurt and being kindly fed. Not even did any dog bark at him.

So the citizens of Gubbio maintain today, but in La Verna, not far away, they will tell you that Brother Wolf was in fact a brigand named Lupo, who would put his victims on a rock pinnacle, remove the plank used for access, and leave them to die of hunger or pay ransom. All this wickedness was ended by Francis's intervention.

Francis's love was not limited to birds and beasts. When he had the chance he would throw fresh-caught fish back into the water, urging them not to let themselves be taken again. A cicada made its home beside the Master's cell, and sang there lustily. Francis summoned the creature; it settled on his hand. Said Francis: "Sing, Sister Cicada, and by your joyous stridulations praise the God who made you." Whenever Francis left his cell he would tickle the insect and bid it sing. And sing it did, for a full week. Then he ordered it to begone, for fear that he might make of his conquest a pretext for vanity. He spent a full day watching bees at their work and applauding their industry. (But he did not like ants, which work too long and hard.) He gave bees honey and wine to sustain them in winter. He would pick up worms on the path and set them aside, lest they be crushed. He loved flowers, and preached to the spring fields in bloom. He insisted that space be left in the kitchen garden for flowers, which proclaim the beauty of the Father and suggest the perfume of eternal suavity. He said: "Every creature cries

aloud: 'God made me for thee, O man!' " He loved the
living woods, and ordered his woodcutters merely to trim
trees, not destroy them. The trees, he said, should remember Jesus, dead on their cross. He was fascinated by
fire, and would not allow it to be roughly extinguished.
Water he loved also, especially in running brooks; he
walked reverently on stones. On washing his hands, he
was careful not to spill water where a foot might tread
on it.

Curiously, this lover of all life did not take the next
logical, almost inevitable, step and refuse to eat meat. It
was indeed the brothers' custom to accept any food
offered them, with small regard for fast days. Francis, ill,
called for a chicken leg, for a kind of ragout, or stew, for
a pig's foot. In the last instance, simple Brother Juniper
attacked a herd of swine with a kitchen knife, cut off a
foot, and served it to the Master. Francis ate it with gusto;
he expressed the utmost sympathy with the robbed swine-
herd, uttering dolorous cries, but none for the squealing
bloody-stumped three-legged pig. Francis hardly attained
consistency, a precarious state.

Of Francis's ability to lure birds and beasts there can
hardly be any question. But the modern reader may well
inquire as to the nature of his alluring power and may
ask science for an explanation. Unfortunately science
seems to refuse a comprehensible answer, or she hides it
in inaccessible periodicals. Of course, men have been
talking with the birds since the time of King Solomon,
and modern ethologists aplenty penetrate their intimate
lives. Konrad Lorenz's goslings follow him, quacking:
"Mama! Mama!" and he quacks back in their language.
And Indian fakirs pipe to their swaying cobras, and commercial moosecalls summon amorous moose, and orni-

thologists with tape-recorded bird voices befool the birds. But the scientists deny that they have any magic faculty, mesmeric power, or radar or smell; they say they depend on free food and immobility and patience; especially patience. Animals, they say, are very inquisitive creatures. Sit quiet and barely move, they say, and. the wild things will come to find out what is going on. An outdoor painter of my acquaintance has been bothered on three continents by cows and horses and such coming to observe and apparently criticize. Jane Van Lawick–Goodall in Uganda made the chimpanzees her friends by infinite patience, not by any magical gift of communication. And if Francis possessed any secret for attracting his little brothers and sisters he never revealed it. Or perhaps by inference he ascribed his power only to love, which science cannot reproduce under laboratory conditions.

In his dealings with Nature Francis taught a lesson to his world — the lesson that Nature is interesting, says Professor Lynn White, Jr., of UCLA. The world's inhabitants were no longer to be regarded as merely moral lessons for man. "Now both were autonomous entities. Saint Francis was the greatest revolutionary in history; he forced man to abdicate his monarchy over creation, and instituted a democracy of all God's creatures. Man was no longer the focus of the visible universe." Professor White soberly proposes that Francis be declared the patron saint of ecology.

THIRTEEN

Finale

IN JUNE 1225 THE PAPAL COURT, chased by a popular uprising in favor of a change of popes, removed with unseemly haste from Rome to Rieti, halfway to Assisi. It chanced that a celebrated oculist accompanied the court. Cardinal Ugolini, reminded of Francis's troubles, urged or commanded the Poverello to come to Rieti for treatment. So he was put on an easy-ambling steed and transported from the Portiuncula to Rieti, fifty miles distant. He wore a capacious cowl with a linen-lined woolen veil to shield his eyes from the June sun.

When still three miles from his destination, Francis came to the country church of San Fabiano, and was greeted by a throng of Rieti's citizens, all eager to touch him and if possible to tear off a bit of his clothing as a miraculous souvenir. The unhappy priest of San Fabiano saw his promising vineyard trampled to destruction, and went wailing to the holy man. Francis promised him that he should not suffer, and indeed when the vintage came the vineyard yielded double its normal crop. This was not much of a miracle, as miracles go, but it well illustrates the trials of sainthood.

To gain peace and solitude, Francis soon retreated to the high inaccessible hermitage of Fonte Colombo. His health grew steadily worse. His bloodshot eyes, distressed by weeping, caused him constant pain. The usual remedies, salves and emollients, cataplasms and callyria, proved vain. The eminent oculist concluded that he must proceed to cauterization. He prepared a bed of hot coals and placed his iron thereon until it turned red. The attending friars wept and shuddered. Francis made over the glowing iron the sign of the cross and said: "Brother Fire, surpassing in beauty, the Most High made you mighty, lovely, and useful above all things. Be kindly to me in this hour, be gentle, for I have always loved you in the Lord. I pray the Lord who made you to temper your ardor, that I may bear your burning." The doctor traced with his iron a line around the more affected eye, and a line from ear to eyebrow. At the smell of burning flesh the attendants turned to flee. "O ye of little faith," said Francis, "why do you run away? I assure you that I felt nothing. If it were necessary you might do it again." His words were soon put to the test. The specialist cut the veins above his temple and bled him copiously. And as this treatment seemed to avail nothing, the patient was transported to the bishop's palace in Rieti and another oculist was called. He was shocked at the first doctor's treatment, and endeavored to correct it by piercing both the patient's ears with a red-hot iron. But this did no good either.

Too weak to talk or think, Francis spent the winter of 1225–1226 in Rieti or in one of its nearby hermitages. In the spring, somewhat recovered, he was carried to

Siena to consult another medical eminence, whose efforts also proved to be vain. To his other woes were added the pains of dropsy, swelling his stigmatized hands and feet. He longed for home, for his brothers at the Portiuncula. Under the tender conduct of Brother Elias he was borne there, presumably in a litter between two horses who had no consideration for the sick. The party, with armed guards, made a wide detour around Perugia, which might well seize the holy man to exploit his remains, certain to work miracles. Assisi welcomed him with an explosion of joy, for, says Tommaso da Celano ingenuously, "everyone hoped that the Blessed One would die soon; that was the cause of their joy."

The precious body was not allowed to rest long in the Portiuncula. To escape the summer heat his guardian, Brother Elias, had him removed to the mountain hermitage of Bagnara, twenty miles to the east. When he had some respite from pain he dictated letters, one to all believers, pointing to significant passages in the Bible, one "to all mayors and consuls, judges and governors throughout the universe," exhorting them to piety. There were other letters to his brother friars. Also he composed a character portrait of the ideal head of his brotherhood. The portrait is, naturally, a self-portrait.

Finally, Francis dictated his Testament. This is more a message than a last will in our sense, for obviously he had nothing material to leave his friends. The Testament begins with a reminiscence of his youthful horror of lepers and of his conquest of that repulsion. He declares then his total submission to all ordained priests. "I don't want to discern sin in them; for what I perceive in them is the Son of God; they are my lords." They are blessed, as custodians of Christ's body and blood. The holy names are to be jealously guarded; any scrap of writing must be saved, as it may contain a sacred name, even in scrabbled form. He then recalls the happy time when the brothers worked together, refusing pay; and he enjoins them in the future not to accept churches or fine residences, for the friars are only transient guests on earth, strangers and sojourners here. They are not to make any pleas or representations to the Roman Curia (contrarily to his own practice, by the way). He pledges obedience to the minister general and to any supervisor placed over him. And he stipulates that any brother who may fall into heresy or disobedience shall be imprisoned and turned over to the cardinal of Ostia for disciplining. And no one is to add to or subtract a jot from these words.

The Testament is often described as a manifesto against the innovators within the order, but it is hard to recognize in it more than a collection of random reaffirmations. Similar to the Testament and set down probably at the same time, for the chapter meeting of May 1226, is a letter of instructions for all good Franciscans. It includes some characteristic advice to ordained clerics for the reading of the mass. He begs them "to celebrate their office in the presence of God without concern for the melody of the voice but rather with concern for the concord of the spirit, so that the voice may be in accord with the spirit and the spirit with God."

As summer waned, Francis was brought down from his mountain retreat at Bagnara and established, for security reasons, in the bishop's palace of Assisi. The palace was guarded night and day by a detail of armed citizens. In comfort and well tended, he displayed a kind of feverish cheer, so that his friends murmured: "How can he be so gay when about to die?" A doctor friend from Arezzo came to visit him. "And what is your opinion, Doctor?" said Francis. The physician, embarrassed, replied: "Brother, by God's grace everything will be all right." And Francis: "Tell me the truth, brother; what do you prognosticate? Don't be afraid, for thank God I am no coward afraid of death. The Lord, by His grace and bounty, has bound me so close to Him that I am as happy to live as to die." The physician answered: "Father, according to medical science your illness is incurable; you will die at the end of September, or on the fourth of October." Then blessed Francis, lying helpless on his bed, spread wide his arms and raised his hands to the Lord, exclaiming joyfully: "Welcome, Sister Death!"

He summoned Brothers Leo and Angelo and bade them sing "The Canticle of the Creatures." At the end he said: "I have another stanza for you:

> *And Death is our sister, we praise Thee for Death,*
> *Who releases the soul to the light of thy gaze;*
> *And dying we cry with the last of our breath*
> *Our thanks and our praise."*

He led the others in the singing, tremulously indeed, but with a kind of hysterical mirth, which struck Brother Elias as unseemly. "Father," he said, "you know that the citizens have great faith in you and think you a holy man. They may think that now you should be brooding on death and weeping instead of singing. Remember that your singing can be heard by many within and without the palace, for it is guarded by many soldiers, who might gain an unfortunate impression." (Thus Elias played the familiar role of the cautioner, crying: "What will people say?") Francis replied that his death was at hand, as was predicted, and that he had been directly and divinely assured of his salvation. "Since I have received this revelation I have been so filled with joy that I can no longer weep. And so I sing and I shall sing to God's honor, for He has given me the benefit of His grace and the assurance that I shall share in the bliss of Paradise."

But soon afterward his sufferings were renewed, more acutely. At one moment he was presumed to be dying. The brothers assembled by his bed to receive his last blessing. Sightless, he laid his hand on the head of the kneeling figure at his right side.

"Who is this?"

"Brother Elias."

"That is as I wish. I bless you, my son, in all your deeds, and through you I bless all the brothers. . . ." He continued with his benediction, his forecasts of coming troubles, his warnings. They are too detailed, too literary, to be convincing. "Great trials threaten you; tribulation is at hand. Happy are those who will persevere, despite scandals which shall cause many to stumble." The reporter, Tommaso da Celano, was surely drawing on his acquaintance with the tribulations and scandals, for when he wrote they had mostly died away.

After the deathbed farewell came an anticlimax. Instead of dying, Francis felt a slight false renewal of strength. He insisted that he would not die in any palace; he must be returned to the holy discomforts of the Portiuncula. Brother Elias, who had insensibly assumed control of everything, consented, and the city supplied an imposing armed escort.

Halfway to its destination the track crossed a hillock whence the city and its background of mountains could be seen. Francis recognized the spot and commanded a

"Wait till Sunday, for then I shall be dead, and you can go home with the others."

She waited, with her children and attendants. Francis was feverishly gay, and sang "The Canticle of the Creatures" in a wavering voice. On Friday, before his assembled faithful, he had a loaf of bread brought him. He tried to break it, like Christ in the upper room, but his stigmatized hands were too weak. Others distributed the crusts. "Take, eat; this is my body. . . ."

On Saturday, October third, he was clearly near his end. He asked the doctor to announce the arrival of Sister Death, "for," he said, "she will open for me the door of life." Following his instructions, the brothers laid him on a coarse cloth spread on the ground and sprinkled him with dust and ashes. His voice muttered faintly the 141st psalm,* "I cried unto the Lord with my voice." He struggled to sing once more his "Canticle of the Creatures." But his voice failed. He died singing the praise of death. "He had the look of a smiling saint," said a spectator.

The Lady Giacoma took him in her arms, figuring the Pietà, the Deposition from the Cross.

A great swarm of larks assembled, long filling the air with welcoming music. A frair averred that he saw Francis's soul, a blazing star, borne on a white cloud to heaven.

Before dawn on Sunday, October fourth, the brothers, clerics, and dignitaries gathered together. Guarded against saintrobbers, they marched toward Assisi, carrying the body of their Master and singing hymns appropriate for the dead. Where the road begins its climb toward the city gates the procession turned aside to San

* The 142nd psalm in the Protestant Bible.

Damiano. The precious body was set down before the grilled window through which the nuns received the Eucharist, and the grating was removed. Francis had promised Chiara that she should see him once more; he had not told her that he would first see death.

The friars took the holy body from the bier, and held it between their arms to the window for a great space, until Lady Clare and her sisters were consoled concerning him, though they were full and stricken with many sorrows and tears, seeing themselves deprived of the consolations and admonitions of such a father.

Then the body was carried to the Church of San Giorgio, Francis's parish church, where he had gone to school, where he had preached his first sermon. The Basilica of Santa Chiara stands on its site today.

FOURTEEN

Saint Francis

HARDLY HAD FRANCIS'S SOUL flown to heaven (with no stop in purgatory) when control of his order was assumed by those who were eager to accept the burden and competent to bear it. The official protector, governor, and corrector was Ugolino, cardinal bishop of Ostia, member of the high Roman aristocracy, cousin of Pope Innocent III, and himself *papabile*, of papal calibre. One will remember him. He was virtuous, pious, capable, and ambitious. He loved and admired Francis, but thought him too unwordly to be an administrator in this naughty world. During Francis's long absences from the Portiuncula the cardinal dominated the order's affairs. But he seems never to have sympathized with Francis's mystical idealism; he looked to the Church's practical advantage. He had proposed, for instance, a merger of the Franciscans with the Dominicans, which might possibly have strengthened the two orders, but at the expense of their special inspirations. He collaborated on the rules, and drew up one for Chiara's Poor Ladies, imposing "closure" on them to restrict them within their walls, thus robbing them of certain innocent freedoms, such as personal association with Francis. He was elected pope in 1227, taking the name of Gregory IX. He was a good man, a great pope. He altered the character of Franciscanism, whether for better or worse.

The reader should also be acquainted with Brother Elias. He came from Assisi or its neighborhood, where his father was a mattressmaker. He undertook the social climb of the ambitious, became a law clerk, and may have studied law at Bologna. He was regarded as a scholar, even a man of learning. When he was at least thirty he joined the Friars Minor, in what must have been a revulsion against the life of money-getting, or possibly in a devout imitation of Francis's rejection of organized society. But it is not so easy to reject one's self and become a new person. His evident competence commended him to Francis, who sent him to the East in 1217 to convert Syria and Palestine. His success in winning recruits from the established Church to Franciscanism threatened even to deplete the establishment. He was chosen vicar of the order, under Francis, in 1221. As an old legalist he was shocked by the casual anarchy of the friars. Experience and common sense told him that when once Francis was gone his order would fall apart. He loved Francis dearly and tended him in his final illness, receiving his last blessing.

The moment Francis was dead Elias began to put into effect long-meditated projects for reform. With the support of Cardinal Ugolino he had already imposed a year's novitiate on would-be friars and had made the vows irrevocable, thus making discipline possible. Now he ruled that Francis's Testament was not binding, that total poverty was by no means obligatory, that the Holy See might assume possession of houses for the accommodation of the friars, who might also enjoy the use of books, furniture, horses, and even money, through the agency of a lay steward. Elias became minister general of the order in 1232 and a church magnifico, riding a fine horse, employing a personal chef and a dozen servants, and treating the simple brothers with a high hand.

Before Francis's death Elias had privately cherished the vision of a great church in Assisi, to the glory of his master, of his master's Master, and to some degree of himself. With amazing energy and ability he planned and constructed, in only a dozen years, the immense Basilica of Saint Francis in Assisi, with two awesome churches, one above the other, and a part of the Sacred Convent. The structures make the only papal see outside of Rome, with a papal throne and living quarters. The church's magnificence, its mere existence, seemed to the old comrades a direct defiance of Francis's purposes. When a marble box was set up in the church to receive contributions for the building, Brother Leo took a hammer to church and smashed the box. He was jailed and soundly whipped.

Elias's autocratic habit was stimulated by his jealousy of his predecessors in the order. Caesar of Speyer, his former lieutenant, a missionary and scholar, was clapped in a prison, where he died of mistreatment. Bernardo di Quintavalle, Francis's first convert, hid for two years with a poor woodcutter in the high Apennines, while authority hunted him, to bring him to trial for disobedience. At length Elias's presumption became intolerable to his superiors. He fled to the court of Emperor Frederick II, that infidel enemy of the Church, and was excommunicated by his old ally, Ugolino, Pope Gregory IX.

But Elias had won. He had succeeded in suppressing Francis's dearest principles: the obligation of poverty; the immutability of his rule; the refusal of great churches and dwellings; the insistence on freedom of thought and behavior; the predominantly lay character of his order; the distrust of theological scholarship. Elias had achieved the divorce of Francis from Lady Poverty. The Church pronounced the dissolution of the marriage in the bull *Quo elongati* of 1230, which pointed out that Francis had no authority to bind his successors, that ownership of apparent Franciscan property resided with lay trustees, and that "no one is considered to *own* what he merely *possesses,* so long as he does not in conscience *consider* himself as owner."

Were the new directions imposed by Elias good or bad? Bad, say modern writers imbued with the spirit of Francis. Good, say sober historians, alleging that the leaderless order, without Elias, would have disintegrated into a dozen quarreling heresies, to become a quaint example of the disasters of dissent. At any rate, Elias's firmness favored the growth and prosperity of the order, which were further favored by the elevation of Francis to sainthood.

In his lifetime Francis was regarded as a saint by popular acclaim. Italy had need of a powerful advocate in heaven. Emperor Frederick was fomenting uprisings in papal lands. On Easter Day 1228 the Roman mob invaded and upset the high mass of Pope Gregory in Saint Peter's. A story in the *Little Flowers* reveals a common conviction. It appears that God, revolted by human wickedness, proposed to destroy all men and women. "But Christ his Son, praying for sinners, promised to renew his life and his Passion in a man, to wit, in Francis, the Poor Little One and a beggar, through whose life and teaching he would bring back many from all over the world to the way of truth, and many also to repentance." Further, the Mother of Christ promised to renew her virginal purity in a woman, Sister Chiara, to deliver a multitude of women from the devil's clutches. Hence Francis was formally canonized, with the utmost magnificence, on 16 July 1228, only two years after his death.

The country gave its devotion to Saint Francis and, in time, to Sister Chiara, canonized as Saint Clare. The peasants and city workers showed particular fervor, responding to their saint, who shared their joys and sufferings. The lot of the poor was hard; they were at the mercy of pillaging brigand-soldiers, natural disasters, floods and droughts, crop failures, famines, pestilence, and horrid infections, such as leprosy. Only the saints could bring solace to the afflicted, hope to the despairing. But the great saints in heaven could be reached by prayer and offerings alone, and one could never be sure that they were listening or that they prized the poor little offerings of the poor. Francis and his brothers in their ragged garments came as familiar household saints to humble dwellings. Francis himself said that his purpose was "to strengthen the poor in their weakness by sharing it"—but not, of course, by striving to end or mitigate poverty. By giving dignity to poverty Francis and his companions helped to allay the natural animosity of the poor toward the rich. It has been noted that "the holiness of poverty is very socially useful." True; but Francis gave no hint that he had such a purpose in mind.

The Franciscans preached peace and concord; but

within the order dispute and dissension raged. The old-timers, especially those who had known and loved the living Francis, clung to his ideals and practices, flaunted their poverty and self-castigation, and demanded literal adherence to his rule. This generation passed, and was succeeded by other generations of men (and women), some drawn by their natures to suffering and self-discipline and rejection of the world, others allured by the Franciscan ideal of service but repelled by asceticism as needless or worse. The rigorists were called the Zealots, later the Spirituals, later the Strict Observants. Against them were ranged the Laxists, *Relaxati,* led at first by Brother Elias; and in between, in greatest numbers, the Moderates, or the Conventuals.

The history of the Franciscans must be compressed in a few words. By any worldly reckoning it is a story of success. A century after the founder's death the order possessed — if the word is permissible — 1,500 houses. But unspiritual rancor and ill will brooded often in those retreats. Many Spirituals demanded separation from their nominal brothers. At the end of the thirteenth century a Spiritual publicly denounced the Roman Church as an agent of Antichrist. The rebels built or excavated hermitages and sanctuaries in the mountains, and early in the fourteenth century they formally seceded from their order. Pope John XXII, in Avignon, took severe measures. Many of the dissidents were jailed, and over a hundred were burned as heretics. In 1323 the Church decreed that it is heresy to allege that Christ and his disciples did not possess property. Here was a strange outcome of Francis's wooing of Lady Poverty! What did he, in heaven, think he had done to his followers?

Most of the Spirituals surrendered to official commands

and threats. Some, however, joined the Fraticelli, a frankly heretical sect that maintained the doctrine of Christ's poverty. The Moderates, or Conventuals, proposed to suppress the whole prickly question. But the founder's old passionate affirmations would not be downed. Following generations read their order's classics and were moved to dangerous thoughts. A new movement uprose, favoring asceticism and discipline. Its members, the Observants, throve from the fourteenth century on. The order as a whole came to befriend scholarship, philosophy, and science. It produced a galaxy of supreme scholars, among them Roger Bacon, Duns Scotus, William of Occam, and Saint Bonaventure. Eventually the controversies within the order died down, and the divisions were finally healed in 1897.

The special mark of Franciscanism today is its concern with the poor, the suffering, and the benighted who have never heard of Christ. Its missionary work in Egypt, the Levant, China and elsewhere has been active and beneficent. It works particularly with the city poor, and is by them beloved. Its popularity has, however, awakened hostility and jealousy. When wandering evangelists visited a lonely village or a poor city parish they would whip up evangelistic excitement, parade virtuous behavior beyond the reach of the local incumbent, correct his Latin, and demand a physical cleaning of his church. If priests, they would hear confessions. They were popular confessors, for a peasant does not like to confide his sins to a fellow peasant, priest or no, perhaps a blabber in his cups. The Franciscans were also accused of being overimportunate in their begging. It was said that people feared meeting a friar as they feared to meet a robber.

However, such hostilities are trifling. In general, the

lowly of city and country loved the Franciscans, accepting their simplicity of dress and behavior and their criticism of churchly pomp and pride. But the secular clergy was inclined to look at them askance, accusing them of trying to replace the Church with their own hierarchy and doctrines. Indeed, there was something in the accusation. The emotional mysticism of the Franciscans escaped from the traditional disciplines of the Church. Francis usurped some of the devotion which might otherwise have gone to Jesus. And some enthusiastic brothers, improving on the prophecies of Joachim of Flora, proclaimed that while the first age of humanity was that of God the Father, and the second age that of God the Son, the third age, now dawning, was that of Saint Francis, who was the reincarnation of Christ himself.

With or without the special favor of divinity, Francis's success in the world has been phenomenal. He has about 50,000 vowed followers, Friars Minor, and a great host of Poor Clares, and a multitude of lay Tertiaries, and numberless others, non-Catholic, non-Christian, who have been caught and held by his example and his person.

That magical personality, operative through time and space, demands an effort at definition.

His guiding purpose was the imitation of Christ. Francis, like Jesus, had his twelve apostles, including a Judas who deserted and hanged himself. Francis did his miracles, spoke his parables, endured the devil's temptations, fasted just short of forty days, bore the stigmata, expressed scorn of formalized religion, government, and social structure, ascended, even, into heaven — if we are to believe one bedazzled witness. Said Tommaso da Celano: "He bore Jesus in his heart, Jesus on his lips, Jesus in his ears, Jesus in his eyes, Jesus in his hands,

Jesus everywhere. . . . Everything he said and did seemed to me to exhale God's perfume."

Exhaling God's perfume, he cast a spell on his followers. Some today go so far as to put the imitator of Christ on the same footing as the model. Such adoration surely goes too far. Francis cherished glaring faults and flaws, especially spiritual ambition, spiritual pride. He proclaimed his unworthiness and insignificance, but he demanded that everyone listen. "God has found in me the vilest of creatures," he said. "Hence He has chosen me to confound the nobility, grandeur, strength, beauty and knowledge of the world, so that all may recognize that all good comes from Him." Well, hardly. Francis did not believe for a moment that he was the vilest of God's creatures — or only for a moment. He had too much common sense to imagine that he would confound the nobility, grandeur, strength, beauty, and knowledge of the world. His vanity, his self-assurance, were of cosmic dimensions. He spoke *ex cathedra,* imitating the voice of God. After dictating his *Testament* he said: "Woe to those friars who oppose what I know to be God's will! . . . What afflicts me is their opposition to what I obtain from God's mercy through prayer and meditation." To dramatize his humility he had ashes strewn on his cell floor, then struggled out of his robe and lay naked in them, saying: "I have done my work; may Christ teach you to do yours." He knew that his abasement in this life would be recompensed by a warm welcome and bliss in heaven and by earthly glory after death. He smiled complacently at a friar's description of the silk hangings and baldachins that would surely shroud his tomb.

In his spirit dwelt then a troubling discord of opposites — self-scorn and self-assurance, respect for authority and rebelliousness, contempt for the world's values and an ineradicable snobbishness. (Once he threw himself on the ground and bade Brother Bernardo walk three times on his body, while ejaculating: "Lie there, you oaf, son of merchant Pietro Bernardone!" There speaks his old resentment at his nonnoble birth, his disgust with his father for not providing him with a pedigree, his revulsion against his father's honest labor.)

The troubling opposites appear constantly in his character and personality. They may, however, sometimes be reconciled in the recognition of certain constants. Such was the exercise of his mysterious charm. This must have been something real, a tangible quality, a spiritual force. He disarmed and allured all men and women, or almost all. Birds and beasts yielded as readily to his messages of welcome and love. Death by no means extinguished the charm. Il Poverello is beloved today — not worshiped, beloved — as is probably no other saint in the calendar, and by Protestants and unbelievers as well as Catholics.

Francis was the apostle of the natural. His espousal of poverty was essentially the espousal of a simple, unencumbered life. Since he loved nature, he tried to live in her embrace, to eat of her offerings, sleep on her bosom. Even in the practice of religion he strove for simplicity, naturalness. He disapproved of great churches and rich ornamentation, and he was careless of the liturgical formalities of worship. He gave away his chapel Bible to a beggar woman, and when reproached, replied: "God will be better pleased with the good we shall do this poor woman than with our psalmody in choir." Much as he loved music, he told his brothers not to worry about keeping on key, but to think rather of the concord of the spirit than of that of the voices.

Celebrating nature, he celebrated joy, scandalizing the brothers often by his levity. He justified his gaiety as a defense against the devil's wiles; a gloomy soul is easy prey. He alleged that spiritual joy, inward and outward, proceeds from purity of heart.

But does the celebration of joy and of nature accord with Francis's asceticism, his cruel maltreatment of Brother Ass? One may argue that ascetic practice opens a way to joy, a special, superior joy. We must take the adepts' word for it. But the Three Companions tell us that on his deathbed Francis confessed that he had sinned much against his body. He came to recognize that Brother Ass too is one of God's creatures.

The celebration of joy and of nature blends with the celebration of beauty, natural or contrived. He who was to inspire a great outburst of art displayed no esthetic interest in painting and decoration; but natural beauty he loved and hymned, at a time when it had few conscious worshipers. Of course there must have been plenty of unconscious worshipers, but it occurred to almost none to transform an impulse of pleasure on seeing a flower, an animal, a mountain into an emotional description of the object. Francis's "Song of the Creatures" is a landmark not only of literary history but of the history of esthetics.

To Christian doctrine he brought no novel contribution, only emphases. He had small interest in theology, none in philosophy. For him, as for Jesus Christ, religion was holy love. Love would abolish sin and all the world's evil. Love would reform society, convert infidels, appease sufferings, defeat the devil with his armies. This is excellent, and no doubt true, but it was hardly new. Nor has it staled; it is the theme of many modern evangelists.

He has been hailed as a social reformer, a rebel, a defender of the oppressed against feudal despotism. This is surely excessive. He did not deny the rights of property, although he questioned their applications and misapplications. "The poor ye have always with you," said his Master; Francis never asked why. When he began to demolish the hostel at the Portiuncula he desisted when he was told that it was the property of the city of Assisi. Hearing a serf curse his master for robbing him, Francis gave the poor man his cloak and made him promise not to swear; but he did not reprove the rascally master. He did not attack the system; he blamed evil on the individual sinner. He had no program of social reform, beyond a recommendation that men should be inspired, by love, to practice the Christian virtues. And he did not accept the burdens and responsibilities of the poor. His poverty was a release, bringing him freedom to wander where he would, to confront as he pleased the rich and mighty.

In fact, I am not even sure that he loved the poor and sick. The lepers revolted him; he served them out of spiritual bravado, to discipline his repulsion. Kissing the leper's sores, he kissed his own. But when he had proved the point to himself, he quitted the lazarhouse, leaving the nameless, consecrated monks to carry on their nauseating services to the afflicted. They deserve, in their humble anonymity, a word of praise, even a prayer or two. When Francis joined the beggars in Rome he uttered no word of sympathy for them; they were means to illustrate his own humility. He loved the idea of poverty, not the poor, because he hated the rich and the privileges of wealth. Yet we find him constantly seeking out the rich and mighty, the local nobilities, the princes of the Church, even the pope, even the sultan.

Inconsistencies did not trouble him; he did not notice them. He was a contradiction, a paradox. Unbound by custom or tradition, he could act as if he were the first man in the world. Think of his originalities — the concept of total imitation of Christ, and that of systematic total poverty as a way of life in the world, his intimacy with birds and animals and all nature, his bearing of the stigmata, his enactment of the Christmas crib, the foundation of three novel, enduring orders, clerical and lay, the fathering of Italian poetic literature. Abhorring the pretensions of intellect, he was one of the great innovators of intellectual history.

His originalities have become our commonplaces. But he himself does not become commonplace; rather, as we seek to pin him down, he flees and escapes us. He is the saint of the poor, the simple, the unlettered. But he is also the saint of the subtle, the fastidious thinkers. He is the saint of the devout, who love the Lord, and the saint of the rebellious, who would reject society, success, civilization. He is the saint of naturelovers and of the dwellers in foul ghettos. And chiefly he is the saint of those who need no saint, those who have sensed in him the sweetness of God's perfume. These vow to him not the devotion accorded to Saint Francis, but love for Francis, the Little Poor Man of Assisi.

Easter 1973

Suggestions for Further Reading

Index

Suggestions for Further Reading

FRANCIS WAS A TALKER, not a writer. He was author of only a few poems and of the rules for his order, admonitions to the brethren, his Testament, letters, homilies, and the like. These were dictated to scribes. The Latin versions are gathered in his *Opuscula* (Quaracchi, Florence, 1949). An English translation by Father Paschal Robinson was published by Dent, London, and the Dolphin Press, Philadelphia, in 1906, and a version by Benan Fahy was published by Burns and Oates, London and Chicago, in 1964.

The accredited sources for our knowledge of Francis, on which this book is based, are the following:

1. Saint Bonaventure. *Legenda Beati Francisci.* Rome, Quaracchi, 1898. It has been several times translated into English, notably by Benan Fahy (*The Greater Life of St. Francis,* Chicago, Franciscan Herald Press, 1965).

2. Tommaso da Celano. *Legenda Prima* and *Legenda Secunda.* In Latin: Rome, d'Alençon, 1906. In English, translated by Placid Hermann, as *The First and Second Life of St. Francis* (Chicago, Franciscan Herald Press, 1963).

3. *The Three Companions* (Brothers Leo, Rufino, Angelo). In Latin and English, translated and edited by Rosalind Brooke (Oxford, Clarendon Press, 1970).

4. *Legenda antiqua* (also known as *Legend of Perugia*). Archivum Franciscanum Historicum XV (1922).

5. *The Little Flowers of St. Francis.* Latin version, *Actus beati Francisci et sociorum ejus,* ed. Paul Sabatier. Paris, Fischbacher 1902. Often translated and widely popular. Accessible scholarly edition in English by Raphael Brown (Garden City, N.Y., Image Books, 1958).

6. *Speculumn perfectionis,* ed. Paul Sabatier. Paris, Fischbacher, 1898. In English, *The Mirror of Perfection.* A translation by R. Steele is included in *The Little Flowers of Saint Francis* (Everyman Library, New York and London, 1903 ff.). Another translation, by Leo Sherley-Price, appears in *Saint Francis of Assisi, His Life and Writings* (London, Mowbray, 1959; New York, Harper, 1960).

All the above, with other source materials, appear in French in Théophile Desbonnets and Damien Vorreux, *Saint François d'Assise: Documents, écrits et premières biographies* (Paris, Editions Franciscaines, 1968), an invaluable 1,600-page compilation, helpfully annotated. A selection from the early documents, in Latin, edited by Placid Hermann, was published under the title *Via seraphica* (Chicago, Franciscan Herald Press, 1959).

Biographies and special studies abound. Most precious is the five-volume *Nova vita di San Francesco* (Assisi, 1959) by Arnaldo Fortini, one-time mayor of Assisi, who devoted much of his life to archival research and to celebration of the saint. Many of the old standard biographies seem now antiquated, voicing our grandfathers' prejudices rather than our own. Paul Sabatier's truculent biography (1894) should be read with caution. G. K. Chesterton's *Saint Francis* novel (1923), keen and witty, is nevertheless more revelatory of Chesterton than of Francis. Father Cuthbert of Brighton's *Life* (London and New York, 1912) speaks wisely for the Church. Johannes Jörgensen's *Saint Francis* (London and New York, Longman's, 1912) was and still is valuable.

Of contemporary biographies, most are retellings of the familiar story, depending on the abundant source material and on devout emotion and stylistic graces. Especially to be recommended is John Holland Smith's *Francis of Assisi* (London, Sidgwick and Jackson, 1972), which treats his subject rather as a fallible human than as a saint. But the biography most likely to be useful to the student is Omer Englebert's *Saint-François d'Assise* (Paris, 1947), translated into English by Eve Marie Cooper, and supplied with bibliography, learned notes, appendices, and running commentary by Ignatius

Brady, O.F.M., and Raphael Brown. Published by the Franciscan Herald Press, Chicago, in 1965.

As for the physical and historical background, Lina Duff Gordon's *Story of Assisi* (London, Dent; New York, Dutton, 1900) is still fresh and delightful; and Assisi has not changed much. Maurice Rowdon's *Companion Guide to Umbria* (London, Collins, 1969) is a model of an informal companion and guide. For the history of the time one may consult Antonio Cristofani, *Delle storie di Assisi libri sei* (Assisi, Metastasio, 1902) though with, I fear, little reward. More to the point is Arnaldo Fortini, *Francesco d'Assisi e l'Italia di suo tempo* (Rome, Ente per la diffusione e l'educazione storica, 1968). For the conception and development of the theory of Franciscan poverty, see M. D. Lambert, *Franciscan Poverty* (London, SPCK, 1961).

Index